THE COMPLETE GUIDE TO FLIPPING PROPERTIES

THE COMPLETE GUIDE TO FLIPPING PROPERTIES

Steve Berges

John Wiley & Sons, Inc.

Published by John Wiley & Sons, Inc., Hoboken, New Jersey.

Published simultaneously in Canada.

For general information on our other products and services please contact our Customer Care Department within the United States at (800) 762-2974, outside the United States at (317) 572-3993 or fax (317) 572-4002.

Wiley also publishes its books in a variety of electronic formats. Some content that appears in print may not be available in electronic books. For more information about Wiley products, visit our web site at *www.wiley.com*.

Library of Congress Cataloging-in-Publication Data:

Berges, Steve, 1959–
    The complete guide to flipping properties / Steve Berges.
      p. cm.
    Includes index.
    ISBN 0-471-46331-0 (pbk.)
     1. Real estate business.   I. Title.

HD1375.B429 2003
333.33—dc21

                                                 2003053493

Printed in the United States of America.

10 9 8 7 6 5 4 3 2

CONTENTS

■ Contents ■

■ Contents ■

ACKNOWLEDGMENTS

Much of my life has been profoundly influenced by not one, but two, loving fathers. The first father is the father of my spirit. He is my Heavenly Father. It is with deep humility and eternal gratitude that I acknowledge His hand in all that is good and virtuous in my life. The second father is the father of my body. He is my earthly father. It is with intense love and great respect that I acknowledge his hand in all that is pure and decent in my life.

The principle of parenthood, and more particularly, fatherhood, is an eternal principle. It is a pattern that was established in our premortal existence, continues in our earthly existence, and shall endure throughout our postmortal existence. It is with all the sincerity of my heart that I pray I may continue the righteous and loving pattern of fatherhood previously established to the beloved children who have been entrusted into my care—Philip, Samuel, and Benjamin.

Chapter 1

Introduction

$\mathbb{B}$uying and selling real estate can be one of the most profitable and lucrative investments activities an individual can participate in. There are many approaches to investing in real estate, most of which are centered around various time horizons. On one end of the investment spectrum is the buy-and-hold strategy, where an investor might purchase a property and hold it for many years. On the other end is the buy-and-sell strategy, where an investor might hold the property for only a few months, weeks, or even days. It is the latter of these two strategies that I focus on in this book.

While readers of this book are likely to have broad and diverse backgrounds, you do share one thing in common—that being your interest in real estate and, in particular, your interest in flipping properties. I try to be as thorough as possible since some of you are likely to have little to no experience, while others of you are seasoned professionals searching for that edge. This being the case, those of you who have a great deal of experience may find some of the material to be a bit basic. It is vital, however, that I lay the proper foundation for those who are not as experienced. Many of you have most likely purchased single-family houses at one time or another and have at least a minimal degree of rental property experience.

In Chapter 2, the concept of flipping properties, along with specific types of flipping, is more fully discussed. Then in Chapter 3 we examine the notion of a term I coined in a previous book, *The Complete Guide to Buying and Selling Apartment Buildings:* the *value play.* I love using the value play strategy, as it is the quickest and surest way I know of to build wealth when it comes to real estate. In Chapter 4, we explore several methods you can begin using immediately to locate prospective investment properties, and in Chapter 5, we study in depth the most common methods of determining value and examine the most appropriate one for use in your analysis. Proper understanding of the valuation process will greatly facilitate building your real estate portfolio. Then in Chapter 6, we examine more fully the practical application of the valuation methods described in Chapter 5 by using various financial analysis models that were created to analyze potential purchase opportunities.

Chapter 7 helps you to more fully understand the rules of engagement as they apply to buying and selling properties, as we examine the seven steps of successful negotiating. In Chapter 8, we study the advantages and disadvantages of many of the methods of financing. We also take a look at the key elements of writing a professional business plan, as well as credit scores, underwriting guidelines, and the closing process. Then in Chapter 9, we discuss how you can assemble a winning team of professionals to help you maximize your potential. In Chapter 10, we examine the merits of three keys that will help you to maximize your potential as a real estate investor. Finally, Chapter 11 discusses what I refer to as the three principles of power. These three principles are not just limited to helping you succeed in real estate, but, when properly applied, will benefit you in many aspects of your life and will lead to an increase in your level of fulfillment and happiness.

BACKGROUND

A convergence of events from my own life experiences over the past 20-plus years has provided me with unique insight into the real estate market. Three primary components have contributed to my experience. First and foremost, like many of you, I have bought and sold a number of both single-family and multifamily properties over the years, and I am currently an active investor.

Second, my experience as a financial analyst at one of the largest banks in Texas has provided me with a comprehensive understanding of cash flow analysis. Working in the mergers and acquisitions group for the bank, I reviewed virtually every line item of financial statements of related income and expenses for potential acquisition candidates of numerous banks that we had an interest in at any given time. I spent several hours a day using a sophisticated model and a specific set of assumptions to determine the market value of these banks. Since leaving the bank some years ago, I have developed my own proprietary model that I now use to facilitate the valuation process for single-family, multifamily, and development opportunities. The beauty of understanding cash flow analysis is that once you grasp the concept, it can be applied to anything that generates some type of cash flow, whether it be banks, single-family houses, manufacturing businesses, or retail outlets. The type of business is not important provided you understand the key assumptions relative to the specific industry you are evaluating. Finally, my experience as a commercial mortgage broker has provided me with an inside look at the lending process and, more specifically, what the lenders' underwriting departments typically require to get a loan approved.

I believe the culmination of my own skill sets and life experiences will be of great advantage to you as you seek to enlarge your personal real estate portfolio. I should mention one additional characteristic of mine that I attribute more to my personality than to any other factor. It is my inability to be satisfied with any single real estate purchase or acquisition. In other words, the traditional process of buying and holding a property, quite frankly, bores me. Who in their right mind wants to buy a piece of real estate and then just sit on it for 10 or 20 years? I know, I know—a lot of people do, including some of you, I'm sure. As for me, however, I can't sit still long enough to hold an investment that long. I am more of a trader of sorts, or as that applies to real estate, a *flipper.* My personality is much better suited to buying, creating value, selling, and then doing it all over again. It is the thrill of the hunt that I most enjoy. It is finding that next deal, then exploring every possible way to maximize the value of it. In all honesty, I really don't even care for the work and the repairs that are often required to add value to the property. I prefer to delegate as much of that part of the process as possible to those whose skills are more closely suited to those types of activities.

REAL ESTATE: A SOUND INVESTMENT

The concept of buying and selling real estate properties, or *flipping,* is indisputably one of the surest means for the accumulation of wealth. Although the strategy involving flipping is itself short term in nature, let me emphatically state that this is *not* a get-rich-quick book. I am not aware of any so-called get-rich-quick books that are worth the price paid for them. Garnering a sizable real estate portfolio is a process that can take anywhere from a few years to many years. The patient and diligent investor who applies a well-defined and systematic approach over time will enjoy a high probability of earning above-average returns for his or her efforts. As a real estate investor, the fruit you enjoy, however, is directly related to the amount of effort put forth on your part. One is unquestionably a function of the other.

Just as a beautiful and healthy tree requires sunlight, food, and water for proper nourishment, so does the process of building wealth. Leave your fortune to chance, and chances are you will have no fortune to leave. To build wealth, you must plant the proper seeds and then nourish them with food and water over time. An occasional pruning will also be required. Almost before you realize it, a strong and magnificent tree will begin to take shape right before your very eyes. Although the grand and noble oak tree exhibits towering beauty and strength above the surface of the earth, it is the tree's root system, extending deep beneath the surface and unseen by human eyes, that gives it the ability to withstand the mighty forces of nature. Like the oak tree, you, too, must be well rooted in fundamentally sound principles of real estate before your branches can grow. As you apply the principles you learn from this book, you will eventually be able to enjoy a sweet comfort from the shade that your branches will provide. Although the winds of adversity may descend on you with great vigor, if you are prepared, they shall not prevail.

To be successful in real estate does not happen by chance. You must have a well-defined plan outlining your specific objectives. Determine exactly what it is you want out of your real estate investment activities and identify your time horizon for accomplishing your goals. Be realistic as well as specific about your objectives. You must begin with the end in mind. In other words, you must know where you are going before you can begin the journey to your destination. If you don't know where you are going, how will you know when you get there? I recently traveled to Manhattan Island in New York for a business meeting on Wall Street just down from the New York Stock Exchange. Since I had never been to New York before, the first thing I did was to map out a plan for my trip. I began with the end in mind. The end, the twenty-second floor of 67 Wall Street, New York City, New York, was my specific objective. Since I knew that was my destination, it was simple enough to map out a precise plan on how to get there from my point of origin. Inasmuch as I was well prepared, when the day for the trip arrived, I was able to travel directly to the city and arrive well ahead of my scheduled time. Only you can determine your destination in life. If you don't have one, then you'll end up exactly where you intended to go, which is nowhere.

You must carefully analyze each property you consider for investment. You cannot afford to shoot from the hip. Proper analysis requires more than a simple review of the property's physical condition and location. To be successful in this business, you must use a comprehensive approach. This book is intended as a guide to help you develop a format for a complete analysis of each property you consider for flipping. This format, when properly applied, will provide you with a significant competitive edge for the simple reason that most investors do not have a system in place. They may have bits and pieces of a system that they use from time to time, but that is usually the extent of it. By following the guidelines in this book you will no longer arbitrarily buy and hold or buy and sell, but rather, you will truly understand the keys to successful real estate investing. By the time you are finished reading this book, you will know when to pass on a deal and when not to, and even more important, you will know *why*. You will have a better understanding of the principles of valuation and how to apply them to your specific market. Proper understanding of this single principle can be the difference between success and failure. Use the tools at your disposal to make prudent business decisions, and real estate will prove to be one of the best and most sound investments you will ever make.

LEVERAGE: THE OPM PRINCIPLE

Most likely you are already familiar with the OPM principle: *other people's money*. Your objective is to control as much real estate as possible while using as little of your own capital as possible, and this means that you have to use other people's money. The name of the game in this business is leverage. The more of it you have, the more property you can control. Borrowed money can come from many sources, including traditional sources such as a bank, a family member, a business partner, or even the seller (carrying back a note in the form of a second).

Another popular source of borrowing is to use a home equity line of credit (HELOC). Still another is using a line of credit against credit cards. I don't know about you, but I get several offers a week from various credit card companies, oftentimes offering credit of $10,000 or more. In a favorable interest rate environment, there is nothing at all wrong with using these cards as a source of financing for your investments. Be careful though! Don't get caught in the credit card trap by maxing out your cards on consumer goods. In addition, make sure that you have structured the purchase of your property in a manner that will allow you to service the debt on it, whatever the source of that debt is. Debt is a wonderful tool, but, as with any tool, you must exercise caution and respect when using it. Otherwise, you can quickly find yourself in trouble. You must be in control of your debt and manage it wisely. Do not allow your debt to control you.

Whatever the source of your funding, the idea is to use as little of your own money as possible, because that is what your returns are based on. Your return on investment, or cash on cash return, is derived from the simple ratio of the net cash left over after all expenses have been paid over the amount of your original investment plus any out-of-pocket improvements or expenses that require an additional owner's contribution. In a very simple example, if you paid all cash for a $100,000 house that generated $6,000 of income, your return on investment is 6 percent. You might as well leave your money in the bank and save yourself the time and energy that investing in real estate will require. On the other hand, if you invested only $10,000 in the deal and borrowed, or leveraged, the remaining $90,000, assuming the same $6,000 of income, your return on investment now jumps to 60 percent. That's how the concept of leverage works. It allows you to take a little bit of your own money and maximize the return on it.

A number of popular books explain how to apply no-money-down techniques. Many of them are well written and have sound principles. While I am a firm believer in the use of other people's money, in my opinion these methods carry the concept of leverage to an extreme. That's not to say that they don't work. I'm sure in many cases they do. By relying solely on these techniques, however, you are restricting yourself to a much more limited pool of properties from which to choose. Let's face it. You are in the real estate business to make money, and time is money. Why spend all of your time trying to find a no-money-down deal when there are far more houses that can easily be purchased with 5 to 10 percent down? I realize that some of you may not have even that much to start with; if that is the case, then you may have to search for that nothing-down deal. I would encourage you to build as large a capital base as possible so that you can quickly and easily purchase some of the more attractive properties as they become available. For every one or two nothing-down deals that are available, there are at least a hundred deals that can be purchased with 10 percent down. The pool of investment properties available is much larger at this level. In the end, having more choices means greater opportunity, which can potentially mean much more money, and that's why you're in the real estate business, right?

ECONOMIC HOUSING OUTLOOK
FOR THE NEXT DECADE

I recently attended the American Housing Conference in Chicago. Although the theme of the conference was centered around mergers, acquisitions, and valuation methods, Dr. David Berson, vice president and chief economist for Fannie Mae, was there to present the *Long Term Economic, Housing & Mortgage Outlook to 2010*. In his presentation, Berson noted several key points with respect to a favorable outlook for the housing industry as a whole over the next decade.

Berson's forecast calls for average real gross domestic product (GDP) growth of 3.4 to 3.5 percent, versus 3.2 percent during the 1990s (see Table 1.1). In addition, his forecast for fixed-rate

Table 1.1   Historical and Projected Economic and Housing Activity

	1980s	1990s	2000s
Real GDP growth	3.2%	3.2%	3.4–3.5%
30-year FRM rates	12.3%	7.9%	7.2–7.5%
Housing starts	1.48 million	1.41 million	1.64–1.68 million
New home sales	0.61 million	0.73 million	0.91–0.93 million
Existing home sales	2.98 million	4.21 million	5.50–5.64 million
Mortgage originations	$325.5 billion	$934.6 billion	$1,599.4–$1,808.1 billion

Sources: Commerce Department, Federal Reserve Board, HUD, National Association of Realtors, Fannie Mae Economic Projections.

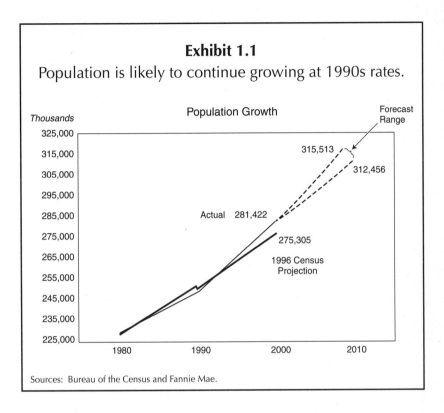

Exhibit 1.1

Population is likely to continue growing at 1990s rates.

Thousands — Population Growth — Forecast Range

Actual 281,422

315,513

312,456

275,305

1996 Census Projection

Sources: Bureau of the Census and Fannie Mae.

mortgages is 7.2 to 7.5 percent, versus 7.9 percent during the 1990s (see Table 1.1). Furthermore, census data for 2010 projects a total population of 315 million, representing an increase of 35 million residents (see Exhibit 1.1). Finally, the national average of unsold homes is at historically low levels, providing for a tight supply-demand relationship (see Exhibit 1.2). All of these factors combine to present an extremely positive outlook for real estate investors.

There you have it. The stage has been set. According to Berson, you should be able to enjoy many opportunities over the next decade to successfully participate in one of the most exciting

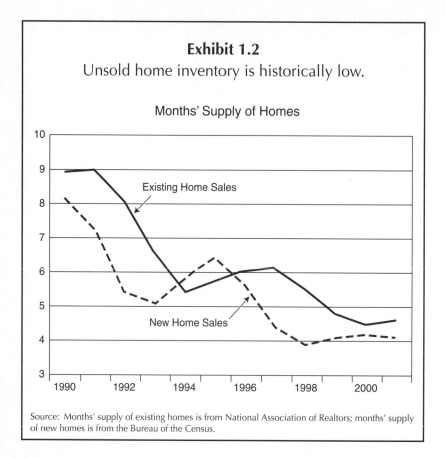

Exhibit 1.2

Unsold home inventory is historically low.

Months' Supply of Homes

Source: Months' supply of existing homes is from National Association of Realtors; months' supply of new homes is from the Bureau of the Census.

industries of all, the real estate industry. The methods outlined in this book enable you to effectively and profitably capture a portion of the many profits that will be generated over the coming years. It is up to you to use the tools provided herein to achieve the level of success you desire.

> What lies behind us and what lies before us are tiny matters compared to what lies within us.
> —*Ralph Waldo Emerson*

Chapter 2

Flipping Properties Defined

$\mathbb{W}$hile there are a number of strategies and techniques used to invest in real estate, there is one thing they all share in common—the element of time. Most investors have some idea of the length of the holding period for properties they intend to acquire. Time can have a significant impact on the growth rate of your real estate portfolio. Time affects such things as the tax rate applied to your gain or loss. The long-term capital gains tax rate has historically been more favorable than the short-term tax rate. Time is also the variable in the rate of inventory turnover. Large retailers are willing to accept lower profit margins on items they merchandise in exchange for a higher inventory turnover rate. Would you rather earn 20 percent on each item or house you sell and have a turnover rate of 1, or would you rather earn 8 percent on each item you sell and have a turnover rate of 3? Let's do the math.

$$\text{Turnover ratio} = \frac{\text{turnover}}{\text{years}} = \frac{1}{1} \times 20\% = 20\% = \text{total return}$$

or

$$\text{Turnover ratio} = \frac{\text{turnover}}{\text{years}} = \frac{3}{1} \times 8\% = 24\% = \text{total return}$$

This simple example clearly illustrates that an investor can accept a lower rate of return on each property bought and sold and earn a higher overall rate of return provided that the frequency, or turnover rate, is increased. I should mention that this example does not, of course, take into consideration transaction costs. These costs may or may not be significant depending on your specific situation, but they must be factored in when analyzing a potential purchase.

Long-term investors may purchase real estate properties and keep them in the family for generations. They will typically hold them for a minimum of five years. Long-term investors seek gains through capital appreciation by simply holding and maintaining their investments while making improvements on an as-needed basis. They often seek to minimize the associated debt and maximize the cash flow. Long-term investors are quite often not fully leveraged. They generally prefer the positive cash flow over being excessively leveraged. When the property is finally sold, the more favorable long-term capital gains tax rates will apply. In addition, long-term investors may or may not elect to take advantage of deferring the tax liability indefinitely through a provision outlined in the Internal Revenue Code, referred to as a *1031 exchange.*

Intermediate-term investors most often hold their properties for at least two years but no more than five years. This class of investor typically seeks gains through a combination of increases in property values resulting from overall price appreciation in real estate, as well as by making modest improvements to the property. Reducing debt to increase cash flow is not as high a priority for intermediate-term investors as it is for their long-term counterparts. This class of investor also tends to be more highly leveraged. Finally, since intermediate-term investors hold their investment properties for a minimum of two years, they are able to take advantage of the lower and more favorable capital gains tax rate.

Short-term investors are defined as those who buy and sell real estate with a shorter duration. They typically hold their investments less than two years. This class of investor most often seeks gains through direct improvements to the property. The shorter holding period does not allow enough time for gains through increases in the overall market. The short-term investor seeks to profit using the higher inventory turnover strategy and may be willing to accept smaller returns, but with greater frequency, realizing the overall rate of return can be considerably higher than with the long-term approach. Since current tax codes penalize short-term investors by imposing higher tax rates on short-term capital gains, they must factor this into their analysis before purchasing any property.

Short-term investors can be further subdivided into different classes. Investors with an extremely short time horizon are known as *flippers* and are the subject of this book. A flipper's primary objective is to locate properties that are undervalued (for any number of reasons), add some measure of value to the property, and then quickly resell it for a profit. Flippers may hold a property for a few months, a few weeks, or even a few days. In some cases, they may not even hold title to the property and may never take possession. This is perfectly legal and can be done through options. The use of options is more fully discussed as we explore the different classes of flippers.

THREE PRIMARY CLASSES OF FLIPPERS

The three primary classes of flippers are the *scout,* the *dealer,* and the *retailer* (see Exhibit 2.1). Each class has its own unique characteristics and serves a valuable function in the world of real estate investing.

Scouts

Scouts serve an important role in the process of flipping and can be very useful to the other two types of flippers, the dealer and the retailer. A scout does exactly what the name suggests—scouts for investment opportunities. Scouts were used many years ago during

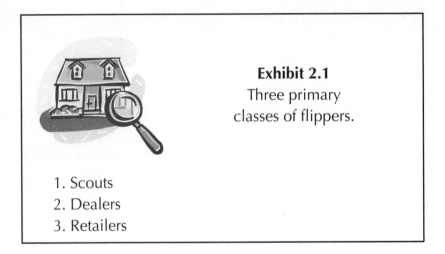

Exhibit 2.1
Three primary
classes of flippers.

1. Scouts
2. Dealers
3. Retailers

the Civil War, as well as other wars, by the United States Army. They were sent out in advance of the troops to gather information about what might lie ahead. The scouts then faithfully and diligently reported back to their captain to disperse key facts gathered during their journey. Important decisions were then made based on the information gathered by the scout. Good scouts were worth their weight in gold. The military today uses a much more sophisticated type of scout, relying on technology such as radar and satellite imagery to report the enemy's position and other vital information. The process itself is much the same though, with key information being provided to those empowered to make decisions.

Just as the scouts in the military report vital information to those who have the power to act on it, so do real estate scouts report key facts regarding potential investment opportunities to dealers and retailers. A good scout will gather as much of the relevant data as possible so that the investors can make well-informed decisions. Scouts provide pertinent information such as the following:

■ General condition of the house or property and its location
■ General condition of the neighborhood

- The price the seller is asking
- The terms the seller is seeking
- The seller's reason for selling
- The seller's time frame for selling and degree of urgency
- Comparable sales for other homes in the neighborhood if possible

Armed with this information, the investor is in a better position to decide whether or not to buy. The dealer or retailer can quickly analyze the data and proceed with a purchase depending on the results of the analysis.

Scouts do not purchase or take legal title to the property. They leave that part of the process to those they report to. Since scouts do not take legal possession, they typically will not be entitled to participate in the profits. This is not always the case, as the individual performing the duties of the scout may belong to a partnership in which the profits are shared. Most often, though, scouts are paid a referral fee, or finder's fee. Just as a real estate agent does not earn a commission unless a sale is made, neither does a scout earn a referral fee unless a deal is consummated. Scouts compensated on this basis will work extra hard to bring you only the best deals. Scouts can be very valuable to investors, as they help them to make the best and most effective use of their time.

Dealers

Much like scouts, dealers also play an important role in bringing opportunities to investors. They often act as wholesalers for retailers and other investors looking to buy property at below-market prices. Dealers are frequently licensed real estate agents and make their money off of the commission and sometimes a slight markup in the price of the property. They know that the markup must be minimal to leave enough profit in the deal to make it attractive to other investors to whom they will sell. Dealers are also in a position to earn money from both sides in the transaction. They are usually both the listing agent and the selling agent. Furthermore, if a dealer sells to a retailer, many times that retailer, after making the required improvements, will turn around and list the property for sale again with the dealer. This provides the dealer with a perfectly legitimate opportunity to double-dip with his or her inventory of listings.

Dealers usually have an extensive network of contacts they work with who provide them with inventory to sell. For example, I know several dealers who have established relationships with various banks' real estate owned (REO) departments, which deal with properties that have been foreclosed on by local banks and remain on their books. The banks are not in the real estate business, but rather they are in the lending business. They have no desire to retain REOs on their books, because REOs represent uncollected loans, or bad debts. Banks prefer to sell these assets and recoup as much as possible. Many times, they will sell the property at the book value of the bad debt—or even below. This practice is not at all uncommon, as most every bank in the country has REOs in its portfolio.

An example of how the real estate owned process works is as follows:

1. Investor A, a novice real estate investor, purchases a rental house for $100,000, puts down $20,000, and borrows the balance of $80,000 from local bank B.
2. After three years of ownership, investor A discovers that the real estate rental business is more difficult than he thought and stops making payments to local bank B.
3. Approximately six months lapse before local bank B is able to repossess the rental house, which it doesn't want and will gladly sell.
4. Local bank B calls dealer C for help to get the bad debt off its books, knowing that dealer C has a large pool of investors she works with who will gladly consider picking up an investment at well below market.

5. Dealer C contacts retailer D, who in turn negotiates a deal with local bank B to take it off the bank's hands at a discounted price of $65,000.

Local bank B is happy because it has converted a nonperforming loan into one that is now performing and collecting interest. Dealer C is happy because she earned a commission from the sale of the property. Retailer D is happy because he bought a house at well below market value and will profit handsomely at the time of resell.

Much like the scouts, dealers specializing in REOs do not, in most cases, take title to the real estate. There is no need to, because their primary role is to act as agents representing sellers who desire to dispose of unwanted assets. Buying real estate owned properties directly from banks would create unnecessary transaction costs for the dealer and greatly increase the amount of time expended. It's more efficient for the dealer to act as an agent for the bank, thereby allowing the bank to sell directly to the retailer or investor. Dealers can make up in volume what they may give up in profit margin.

While some dealers specialize in REOs, others focus on the foreclosure market. Buying and selling foreclosures requires that an individual have a working knowledge of that market. While there are a number of good books written on the subject, many investors do not have the expertise or the time to find undervalued foreclosures. Furthermore, they are unfamiliar with the auction and/or bidding process and may lack the resources to purchase properties in this manner. Dealers who understand the mechanics of buying foreclosed properties can easily make a market by wholesaling to their network of retailers. Dealers participating in foreclosures will most likely take title to the property.

Retailers

The concept of retailing involves buying houses, fixing them up by making various improvements, and then reselling them. As the name suggests, retailers purchase properties at wholesale and subsequently sell at retail. They represent the end of the food chain for flippers. The scout and the dealer serve a vital function in bringing opportunities to the retailer, who will then usually flip the property to a more permanent type of buyer, whether it be another investor who wants to hold it as a rental unit or a homeowner who will be moving into the home to use as a primary residence.

Unlike scouts and dealers, retailers most often take title to the property. They typically hold it anywhere from 30 to 90 days while they make any necessary improvements to the property, then offer it for sale to a more permanent type of buyer. Retailers must have more capital available to work with than the scout or dealer. They need whatever funds are required for the down payment, plus additional funds for property improvements. In addition, the retailer must have adequate capital to sustain the property during whatever holding period may be required. The retailer can plan and hope to have the house sold within 30 days after making all the improvements, but in reality it may take up to six months or, in some cases, even longer. Holding costs during this period include the interest on the debt used to acquire the property, taxes, insurance, and utilities. Since the retailer usually takes title to the property and has more capital at stake, his or her level of risk relative to the scout and dealer is significantly higher.

Of the three primary classes of flippers, it is the retailer who stands to gain the most financially. The relationship between risk and reward is in most cases directly correlated. This means that the greater the risk an investor is willing to assume, the greater the potential reward. This application holds true among the classes of flippers. Scouts assume virtually no risk, and their reward is most often limited to a referral fee. Dealers assume a greater degree of risk than do scouts, and they stand to gain substantially more. Risk for retailers is significantly greater than that for scouts and dealers. They most often take title to the property, have a longer holder period, and invest more capital. It is the retailer, therefore, who stands to enjoy the greatest reward from flipping properties.

In Chapter 3, we more fully explore the concept of retailing the *value play way.*

USING OPTIONS TO FLIP PROPERTIES

An *option* is a legal instrument that gives you the right to buy at a predetermined price. This is done millions of times a day in the stock market. For example, investors can buy a call option on MSFT with a strike price of, let's say, $55. As with all options, time, or *t,* is one of the variables that determine the value of an option using the Black-Scholes model. Investors have the right to exercise an option at their discretion within a specified period of time. It is possible that the outcome will be favorable, and it is also possible that the option will expire worthless. So it is with real estate. Investors may enjoy the legal right to buy a piece of property at a predetermined price through the use of options, then turn around and sell their interest in the property without ever taking title to it.

Some of my real estate investment activities include the use of options for the development of new residential construction in single-family-home communities. The name of the company founded by my partner and me is Symphony Homes (www.symphony-homes.com), chosen because of my love for great music. Within this entity, we use options to acquire rights to undeveloped property without ever taking legal title. We do, however, have a recordable interest. We just don't take title, at least not initially.

Just recently, I optioned 28 lots in phase I of a particular community. This gave Symphony Homes a legal interest in the property and the right to acquire all 28 lots at a predetermined price. When we get a purchase agreement to build a new home for a client on one of our lots, we then exercise our option on that lot and take legal title to it. The advantages of using an option in this case are twofold. The first is that if we have difficulty selling new homes to prospective buyers, we are not stuck with the burden and cost of ownership. The only thing we have at risk is our option money. The second reason is that if we were to actually purchase the lots, the sale would trigger an increase in taxes due to a new and much higher assessed value. As the new owners, we would then be obligated to assume the tax liability.

As you can see, options are one of many valuable tools available to the real estate investor who is interested in mastering the art of flipping. Options enable you to gain control of property with very little money down, thereby allowing you to maximize the use of leverage. I recommend, however, that they be used with prudence. Remember that time is one of the variables—when t expires, so does your option. Carefully analyze the market as it applies to your particular investment opportunity to determine that you have a high probability of a favorable outcome before committing your resources.

CLEARLY DEFINED OBJECTIVES

If you are serious about being successful in the real estate industry, you need to establish clearly defined objectives. You need to determine if you are going to be a long-term, intermediate-term, or short-term investor. If you are going to engage in the practice of flipping, will you be a scout, a dealer, or a retailer? Perhaps your real estate investment activities will include a combination of these strategies. Real estate is like any other business with respect to defining your objectives. You must have a business plan in place. Taking the time to do so will help you stay the course. If you don't know where you are going, how will you know when you get there?

Think of an aircraft about to embark on an intercontinental flight to Europe. The pilot will use an established flight plan to chart his course. His navigator will input key coordinates into the aircraft's navigation system. Once in flight, the crew will rely primarily on the plane's instruments to arrive safely at an exact destination thousands of miles away from the point of origination.

Now try to imagine the crew making this same trip with no flight plan whatsoever. They would greatly jeopardize their ability to reach their destination safely. The crew would also place in danger the very people who have hired them fly to Europe, the passengers.

Like the pilot, as a real estate investor you must also rely on an established flight plan. That flight plan will be your plan of attack, your clearly defined objectives, your business plan. Like the pilot of an aircraft who must occasionally adjust course, so will you, too, occasionally have to adjust your course. You cannot afford to undertake a journey in your real estate profession without having some idea of where you want to go. Many people go through their entire lives in a rather random and indiscriminate fashion, with no sense of direction; hence, they end up precisely where they set out to go—nowhere.

The process of proper planning in this business is critical to your success. Yes, you may have to think a little bit, and it will require some effort on your part to formalize your plans, but I can assure you that any time spent developing a plan will greatly contribute to your success. By mapping out your strategy in advance, like pilots who direct aircraft across vast expanses of the earth, you will eventually reach your destination. You may run into a few storms along the way, but like the aircraft, you will ultimately reach your destination safely.

Three primary components that must be considered when defining your objectives are your entry, postentry, and exit strategies. Let's take our pilot as an example. His entry strategy would include the preparation of his flight plan, crew, and aircraft. The captain would take every precaution to ensure that all was in order before departing on his journey. In fact, pilots and their crews (ground crew included) use what is referred to as a *preflight checklist* before each and every flight to make sure that not a single item is overlooked. The checklist takes into consideration everything the pilot will need in order to have a safe flight, including fuel requirements, weight limitations, and maintenance status. The pilot must also be certain that the weather is conducive to his flight. The pilot's postentry strategy begins as soon as he starts the engines. He and the crew are now fully engaged in the process of flying the aircraft and must focus completely on flying the plane to its destination in the safest and most efficient manner possible. The crew may be able to fly directly to their destination if all goes as planned; however, in the event that their radar indicates turbulence ahead, they may be required to alter their course slightly. It is better for them to adjust their postentry strategy by flying around the turbulent weather than to run the risk of flying directly through it. On successfully navigating to the intended destination, the crew members then implement their exit strategy, which includes landing the aircraft at its predetermined destination and unloading the cargo.

Entry Strategy

To define your entry strategy you will need to start by determining what type of property you are looking for, the price range you are considering, and the holding period. Are you going to buy a single-family house, fix it up, and turn around and sell it, or are you going buy a more expensive small apartment building to hold for a number of years? Are you going to use flipping techniques as part of your investment strategy? If so, you must decide if you are going to act in the capacity of a scout, dealer, retailer, or some combination of the three. How do you intend to finance your purchase? You must, of course, take into consideration the investment capital you have to work with. If you don't initially have the adequate resources required for retailing, you may have to start as a scout or a dealer while progressively building up your capital base. The important thing to remember about having a well-defined entry strategy, regardless of what all that may entail, is that like the pilot, you have a predetermined plan based on specific criteria established by you. Since you have already determined factors such as price range, location, financing, and holding period, you will not waste any unnecessary time examining opportunities that do not match your criteria.

Postentry Strategy

While the postentry strategy begins the moment you close on the property, you should have established your specific objectives long before the closing. You cannot wait until after you purchase the property to decide what you are going to do with it. You absolutely must know that before ever spending a single dollar. Your postentry agenda should include things such as property improvements, rental increases, and management changes, if applicable, and lease or sell preparations as required. If you know, for example, that your strategy is to be a retailer and flip properties, the time to procure estimates for the needed improvements is during the inspection period, while the property is under contract, not after it closes. As a prudent investor, you know almost exactly how much it will take to repair the property and make it ready for resale. If you are contracting the work out, then your contractors should already be scheduled and should be ready to start the work the day after your closing. Don't let a week go by before having the painter come out. Have your painter ready to go as soon as you close! Since you want your investment operations to run as efficiently as possible, it is imperative that you plan as much of your postentry strategy in advance as possible.

Exit Strategy

Your exit strategy is probably the most important of the three components. You should specifically define your intentions before you even purchase a property. Whether you are going to hold it short term or long term, you must determine in advance how you will eventually unwind your position in the property. If you are a short-term investor and are going to flip the property, you want to be certain the market is conducive to your planned activities. In other words, is there sufficient demand? Are interest rates going up or down? Or are they stable? If you are going to hold the property for a number of years, these factors are not as critical. If you elect to maintain your interest in the property and choose not to sell, an alternative to consider is refinancing. This will allow you to unlock some of the equity that has accumulated over the years to invest in additional properties. An advantage of accessing your equity in this manner is that you avoid paying any capital gains taxes. As a flipper, however, you will not be as concerned about long-term holding periods, since your objective is to dispose of the property as quickly as possible. You should determine in advance, however, your method of disposal. Do you plan to sell the property yourself or list it with a real estate sales agent? Regardless of the methods you choose, the criteria for your exit strategy should be established long before you invest any of your valuable resources.

Just as the pilot and crew use a comprehensive flight plan to successfully fly their aircraft, so must you, too, use a comprehensive business plan to be successful in your real estate activities. From start to finish, it is important to plan as much of your strategy as possible in advance. Thus, when you are alerted on your radar screen to unforeseen circumstances ahead, you will be able to adjust your course as necessary and complete your journey for a safe and successful landing in your real estate career.

> I would sooner have the approval of my own conscience and know that I had done my duty than to have the praise of all of the world and not have the approval of my own conscience. A man's conscience, when he is living as he should, is the finest monitor and the best judge in all the world.
>
> —*Heber J. Grant*

Chapter 3

The Value Play Strategy

In my experience of working with other investors and previous clients, I have often heard comments like, "Yes, Mr. Berges, I prefer the buy-and-hold approach to investing in real estate. My idea is to buy a property, pay it off, and live off of the income." Sound familiar? While this method of building a real estate portfolio is a valid one, in my estimation it is certainly not the best method. If you have another source of income that is fairly substantial and therefore allows you to make investments in real estate on a periodic basis, then this may be the method for you, or at least the one that you are the most comfortable with. This approach, however, precludes you from maximizing the utility of your investment resources.

In *The Complete Guide to Buying and Selling Apartment Buildings,* I described an aggressive real estate acquisition campaign for apartment buildings based on a term I coined: the *value play.* The value play strategy as it relates to apartment buildings is very similar to the concept of the retailer who flips single-family properties. The primary difference is that the concept is applied to income producing properties on a much larger scale. The fundamental premise of this strategy is based on finding an undervalued apartment building, large or small, creating value through one or more of many mechanisms, and reselling, or flipping, the property. The value play strategy is undeniably one of the quickest and surest methods available to investors to create and build wealth.

Many real estate books embrace the buy-and-hold strategy of building long-term wealth. Proponents of this approach claim that for individuals to retire with a leisurely lifestyle, all they have to do is buy one property a year for, let's say, 10 years, rent the units out, and pay down the debt. At the end of 25 years, all of the debt will be paid off and the investor can live off of the rents. This strategy may work fine for many; some may find that this is all they are comfortable with. But as I will demonstrate, investors who maximize their efforts through use of the value play concept, especially as it applies to the retailer, will end up with far greater wealth than those who implement a simple buy-and-hold strategy.

The financial implications of value-added measures can be quite significant for the retailer. The examples in Tables 3.1 and 3.2 illustrate just how powerful the value play strategy can be. Investor A implements a simple buy-and-hold strategy of acquiring one property a year for 10 years and holds all 10 properties through year 25. He chooses not to sell any of them, but ensures that all mortgages are fully paid by the end of the 25-year period. Investor B implements the value play methodology over the same 25 year period. She, on the other hand, buys and sells two value play properties for each one sold in the prior period for 10 years, with the exception of the last year. In year 10, she retains all properties purchased, which she will keep and maintain through year 25. Like investor A, she will ensure that the mortgage is fully paid by year 25. Take a minute to review the following assumptions and then carefully study Tables 3.1 and 3.2.

BUY-AND-HOLD STRATEGY

Investor A Assumptions

- Investor A saves enough to purchase one house each year for 10 years.
- Each house costs $75,000.

Table 3.1 Investor Strategies

| | Investor A Buy-and-Hold Strategy | | | | | | | | | | |
Year	Unit 1	Unit 2	Unit 3	Unit 4	Unit 5	Unit 6	Unit 7	Unit 8	Unit 9	Unit 10	Combined Values
1	75,000										75,000
2	78,000	75,000									153,000
3	81,120	78,000	75,000								234,120
4	84,365	81,120	78,000	75,000							318,485
5	87,739	84,365	81,120	78,000	75,000						406,224
6	91,249	87,739	84,365	81,120	78,000	75,000					497,473
7	94,899	91,249	87,739	84,365	81,120	78,000	75,000				592,372
8	98,695	94,899	91,249	87,739	84,365	81,120	78,000	75,000			691,067
9	102,643	98,695	94,899	91,249	87,739	84,365	81,120	78,000	75,000		793,710
10	106,748	102,643	98,695	94,899	91,249	87,739	84,365	81,120	78,000	75,000	900,458
11	111,018	106,748	102,643	98,695	94,899	91,249	87,739	84,365	81,120	78,000	936,476
12	115,459	111,018	106,748	102,643	98,695	94,899	91,249	87,739	84,365	81,120	973,935
13	120,077	115,459	111,018	106,748	102,643	98,695	94,899	91,249	87,739	84,365	1,012,893
14	124,881	120,077	115,459	111,018	106,748	102,643	98,695	94,899	91,249	87,739	1,053,409
15	129,876	124,881	120,077	115,459	111,018	106,748	102,643	98,695	94,899	91,249	1,095,545
16	135,071	129,876	124,881	120,077	115,459	111,018	106,748	102,643	98,695	94,899	1,139,367
17	140,474	135,071	129,876	124,881	120,077	115,459	111,018	106,748	102,643	98,695	1,184,941
18	146,093	140,474	135,071	129,876	124,881	120,077	115,459	111,018	106,748	102,643	1,232,339
19	151,936	146,093	140,474	135,071	129,876	124,881	120,077	115,459	111,018	106,748	1,281,633
20	158,014	151,936	146,093	140,474	135,071	129,876	124,881	120,077	115,459	111,018	1,332,898
21	164,334	158,014	151,936	146,093	140,474	135,071	129,876	124,881	120,077	115,459	1,386,214
22	170,908	164,334	158,014	151,936	146,093	140,474	135,071	129,876	124,881	120,077	1,441,662
23	177,744	170,908	164,334	158,014	151,936	146,093	140,474	135,071	129,876	124,881	1,499,329
24	184,854	177,744	170,908	164,334	158,014	151,936	146,093	140,474	135,071	129,876	1,559,302
25	192,248	184,854	177,744	170,908	164,334	158,014	151,936	146,093	140,474	135,071	1,621,674
Income	9,600	9,984	10,383	10,799	11,231	11,680	12,147	12,633	13,138	13,664	255,920

Assumptions for investor A
1. Saves enough to purchase one house per year for 10 years by putting down $7,500, or 10%, on each house
2. Holds each property through year 25
3. Arranges mortgage payments so all units are owned free and clear by year 25
4. Assumes annual growth rate of 4 percent
5. Assumes rental income of $800 per month in year 1 that grows at the annual rate of 4%

Table 3.2 Investor Strategies

Investor B — The Value Play Strategy

Year	Units 1	Units 2	Units 4	Units 8	Units 16	Units 32	Units 64	Units 128	Units 256	Units 512	Combined Values
1	75,000										75,000
2	20%	150,000									150,000
3	15,000	20%	300,000								300,000
4	15,000	30,000	20%	600,000							600,000
5	30,000	30,000	60,000	20%	1,200,000						1,200,000
6	20%	60,000	60,000	120,000	20%	2,400,000					2,400,000
7	150,000	20%	120,000	120,000	240,000	20%	4,800,000				4,800,000
8		300,000	20%	240,000	240,000	480,000	20%	9,600,000			9,600,000
9			600,000	20%	480,000	480,000	960,000	20%	19,200,000		19,200,000
10				1,200,000	20%	960,000	960,000	1,920,000	20%	38,400,000	38,400,000
11					2,400,000	20%	1,920,000	1,920,000	3,840,000	39,936,000	39,936,000
12						4,800,000	20%	3,840,000	3,840,000	41,533,440	41,533,440
13							9,600,000	20%	7,680,000	43,194,778	43,194,778
14								19,200,000	20%	44,922,569	44,922,569
15									38,400,000	46,719,471	46,719,471
16										48,588,250	48,588,250
17										50,531,780	50,531,780
18										52,553,052	52,553,052
19										54,655,174	54,655,174
20										56,841,381	56,841,381
21										59,115,036	59,115,036
22										61,479,637	61,479,637
23										63,938,823	63,938,823
24										66,496,376	66,496,376
25										69,156,231	69,156,231
Income	0	0	0	0	0	0	0	0	0	13,664	13,103,119

Example

Purchase Price	75,000
Value Created Percent	20%
Value Created Dollars	15,000
Original Equity	15,000
Accumulated Equity	30,000
LTV Ratio	20%
Next Purchase(s)	150,000

Assumptions for investor B
1. Starts with initial $15,000 equity
2. Buys and sells two value play properties for each one sold, but holds all properties purchased in years 10 through 25
3. Creates value on each deal of 20 percent
4. Maximizes leverage on each new property purchased using a loan-to-value ratio of 80 percent (or 20 percent down on each deal)
5. Assumes annual growth rate of 4 percent
6. Assumes no rental income except in years 10 through 25

- He obtains a 90 percent loan on each house, which means he puts a down payment on the property of 10 percent, or $7,500.
- Investor A holds each property purchased over the 10-year period all the way through year 25 and does not sell any of them.
- He arranges his mortgage payments to be paid down to zero by year 25. In year 1, he gets a 25-year loan; in year 2, he gets a 24-year loan; and so on. Finally, in year 10, investor A gets a 15-year loan so that all loan balances will be zero in year 25, enabling him to live off the income as planned.
- All properties purchased appreciate in value at an annual growth rate of 4 percent so that by the end of year 25, the 10 units purchased have a cumulative value of $1,621,674.
- The rental income on a house purchased for $75,000 in year 1 is assumed to be $800 per month, or $9,600 for the year. The rental income grows at an annual growth rate of 4 percent so that by year 10, the income per unit has grown to $13,664, and by year 25 the rental income per unit has grown to $25,592, or $255,920 combined income for all 10 units owned.

THE VALUE PLAY STRATEGY

Investor B Assumptions

- Investor B starts with $15,000 of equity.
- Each house costs $75,000. She is able to use the $15,000 of equity for both the down payment and minor improvements that will be required.
- She buys and sells two value play properties for each one she sells, in effect doubling the number of houses bought and sold each year for years 1 to 10. All properties purchased in year 10 are retained in her real estate portfolio.

■ Investor B creates value of 20 percent on each property purchased.

■ She arranges her mortgage financing so that all loan balances will be zero by year 25, thereby enabling her to live off the income.

■ All properties purchased and retained in her real estate portfolio appreciate in value at an annual growth rate of 4 percent so that by the end of year 25, the 512 units purchased have a cumulative value of $69,156,231.

■ The rental income on a house purchased for $75,000 in year 1 is assumed to be $800 per month, or $9,600 for the year. The rental income grows at an annual growth rate of 4 percent so that by year 10, the income per unit has grown to $13,664, and by year 25 the rental income per unit has grown to $25,592, or $13,103,119 combined income for all 512 units owned.

After reviewing Tables 3.1 and 3.2, I think you will agree that the difference between the two investment strategies is quite significant. Using the assumptions outlined in Table 3.1, investor A's buy-and-hold strategy has netted him an equity in the combined properties of $1,621,674. In addition, he will enjoy an annual income of $225,920. That actually sounds pretty good, doesn't it? All he has to do is buy one property a year for 10 years, hold them for 25 years, and he can retire very comfortably. Investor A's buy-and-hold strategy sounds good, that is, until you compare his value with investor B's. Investor B, using the value play strategy, has managed to accumulate a sizable fortune of $69,156,231. Furthermore, she will enjoy a very comfortable annual rental income of $13,103,119. What a fantastic difference between the two! To fully take advantage of the value play methodology, you must have a well-defined plan that you strictly adhere to, and you must be willing to execute it, that is, to take action. This kind of wealth accumulation is possible only through the systematic application of a well-designed plan.

It could be argued that the assumption of 20 percent appreciation is not reasonable, but I can tell you from my own experience
that not only is it reasonable, but it is conservative. A 22-unit
property I purchased, for example, was subsequently sold within
a year for approximately 80 percent more than I paid for it. Creating value in single-family houses is actually much easier to do
than in apartment buildings, and you should have no trouble earning 20 percent or more on your real estate transactions.

It should be noted that Tables 3.1 and 3.2 are, of course, hypo-
thetical tables. The example is used to demonstrate the full potential of an investor who diligently applies the value play strategy,
given certain assumptions, over a period of many years. The volume of units bought and sold in years 1 to 8 is entirely feasible
and quite manageable. In the latter years, in which many more
properties are acquired, the value created of 20 percent or more is
still achievable; however, the sheer volume will be more difficult
to achieve. To buy and sell that many properties in a single year
requires a team of investors working together, with each one performing a unique set of functions. If we were to take Table 3.2 and
reduce assumption 3 for investor B from 20 percent down to 15
percent, the resulting value at the end of year 25 would be
$20,792,360. That still represents a value of wealth equating to
roughly 13 times greater than the wealth created by investor A.
Clearly the value play strategy warrants every investor's consideration.

THE VALUE PLAY SELECTION PROCESS

As you may recall, the retailer is in the business of buying real
estate at wholesale or below and subsequently reselling it at retail.
The principal mechanism that enables the retailer to do this is the
process of creating value through any number of methods. Since
multifamily properties such as apartment buildings derive their
value primarily from the income they generate, there are many
ways to enhance the revenues while simultaneously reducing

expenses to improve the overall net operating income (NOI). The price an investor is willing to pay for an apartment building is almost always a function of the NOI divided by a given capitalization rate for similar income-producing properties. The following illustrates a simplified example of how this valuation formula works.

$$\text{Property value} = \frac{net\ operating\ income}{capitalization\ rate} = \frac{\$100,000}{0.10} = \$1,000,000$$

For the retailer dealing with single-family houses, however, income is not as important because the resell value is based more on market comparables rather than the income it generates. This means that the buying public will evaluate the house you have for sale based on what is currently available in your immediate market. Buyers will compare and contrast your property to many others and will ultimately select the one that best fits their needs. Their buying decisions will be based on factors such as the property's location, its condition, the price at which it is being offered, its proximity to major streets and shopping areas, and the quality of schools in the area. In addition, many personal factors affect the buying decision, such as proximity to work, church, and Grandma and Grandpa's house. Some factors that affect a buyer's decision-making process fall outside the realm of your control, because not all buyers are searching for the same set of conditions that may compel them to choose one house over another.

Three factors that you as the retailer do have some control over, however, include the property's *location,* its *price range,* and its *physical condition.* Although a prospective buyer's needs will vary, you can still make sound investment decisions based on market generalizations. You must recognize that the products you have available to sell cannot, and will not, be all things to all people. Nevertheless, you can make certain assumptions, based on objective data, that will greatly improve your chances of success.

Property Location

As an investor who is in the business of flipping properties, you are not interested in carrying your inventory any longer than necessary. That means you should carefully study your area to determine which vicinities are selling with the fewest average number of days on the market. If you have lived in a particular area for a while, you are likely to already know which areas of town are hot and which are not. You do not have to rely solely on your intuition, however, as most real estate agents in your area will have access to the local Multiple Listing Service, or MLS. They can provide you with objective data to support your analysis. Most real estate agents will gladly furnish this information to you free of charge. They are in the business of earning commissions by representing buyers and sellers, and to do this, they must also be able to provide information that will enable them to make a well-informed decision. Sales agents know that if they can give you the facts you need that will support your decision to buy, it will bring them one step closer to earning a commission.

The type of location best suited for a retailer seeking to flip properties is typically a neighborhood between 10 and 30 years old. These are the neighborhoods in which the average middle-class citizen lives. Neighborhoods less than 10 years old tend to have larger and more expensive homes, which offer fewer retailing opportunities. Neighborhoods older than 30 years often consist of run-down properties in declining areas of town. This is not always the case, of course, as I have seen some areas 40-plus years old that continue to be well maintained and where pride of ownership exists. The 30-year rule is a generalization. The propensity is for homes and neighborhoods older than that to be declining in value, and they may require a longer holding period. (See Exhibit 3.1.)

The ideal location is an area not suffering from functional obsolescence in which the majority of homes are well maintained. Ideally, the neighborhood is established, has good schools nearby, and continues to have homes that sell in a shorter-than-average

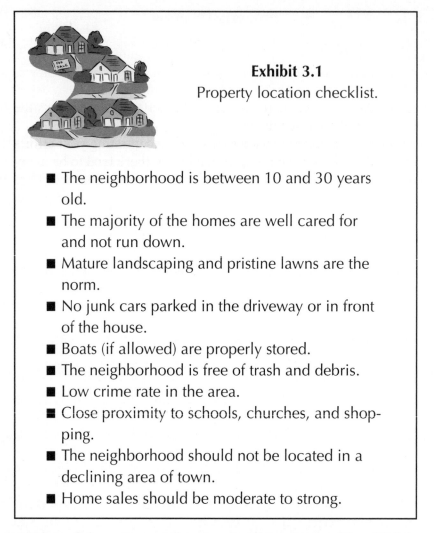

Exhibit 3.1
Property location checklist.

- The neighborhood is between 10 and 30 years old.
- The majority of the homes are well cared for and not run down.
- Mature landscaping and pristine lawns are the norm.
- No junk cars parked in the driveway or in front of the house.
- Boats (if allowed) are properly stored.
- The neighborhood is free of trash and debris.
- Low crime rate in the area.
- Close proximity to schools, churches, and shopping.
- The neighborhood should not be located in a declining area of town.
- Home sales should be moderate to strong.

number of days compared to surrounding communities. Visible characteristics often include mature landscaping, pristine lawns, and well-cared-for homes. What you are looking for is a home in obvious need of repair in a community such as this. The grass is often overgrown, the house looks run down (and usually is), and the neighbors shake their heads in disgust as they pass by. Believe me, they are waiting for someone just like you to come along and get rid of that eyesore in their neighborhood!

Price Range

Most opportunities for flipping properties are at the lower to middle end of the price range. The lower end of the price range is, of course, relative to your area. In California and New York, it may be $250,000, while in Texas $75,000 to $100,000 represents the lower end of the price range.

There are three primary reasons for concentrating your efforts in this price range. The first reason is that there tend to be many more opportunities available. Homes selling in this price range tend to be older and are frequently in greater disrepair than newer and more expensive homes. The second reason to focus on the lower to middle end of the price range is that there is a larger pool of buyers available to purchase these types of homes. Many prospective buyers in the lower price range are younger couples, who may be first-time buyers, or working-class people simply looking for affordable housing. The higher up the price scale you go, the smaller the pool of buyers. Finally, homes in this price range are easier for you as the investor to afford. Why tie up your capital in larger, more expensive homes that are harder to resell when you can buy smaller, more affordable homes? In addition, if you have a limited amount of investment capital to work with, financing will be easier to obtain on less expensive homes.

Physical Condition

A property's physical condition can range from extremely poor, as in condemned, to very good. Your focus should be on those properties that fall somewhere in between. This category will prove to be the most profitable, as you will be able to minimize the amount of capital required for improvements, thereby allowing you to maximize your return on investment. Another key consideration is the time involved in making the more extensive repairs. The turnaround time for houses that require only minor repairs is much shorter than for those that require major repairs. A thorough understanding of what to look for is key to your success in this business. Ideally, you want to find properties that look a lot worse than they really are. In other words, you are looking for houses that are in need of cosmetic-type repairs such as new paint, landscaping, and perhaps a good, thorough cleaning. Cosmetic repairs are quick and easy to make and are often the least expensive.

While properties in extremely poor condition can frequently be purchased at bargain-basement prices, they will typically require much more money for improvements. When it comes to houses, cheaper is not necessarily better. The initial price may be much less than other homes in the area, but the time and resources required for property improvements will often outweigh any advantage gained from the purchase price. Houses that fall into this category are usually in need of major repairs, which can be quite expensive.

The following inspection items are things to look for in your assessment of a property's physical condition. For a more comprehensive checklist, please see Appendix A, "Property Inspection Check List."

A bad foundation is one problem that can be very costly to repair. If the house is built on a concrete slab where major settling has occurred, the house will have to be leveled. Leveling a house can be very costly, and it can also be time-consuming. Furthermore, houses with foundation problems are likely to have other structural damage caused by the settling. A close inspection of the interior walls will almost always show evidence of settling, as the drywall will crack and separate. It is common to see hairline cracks in walls, especially around the seams, so don't be alarmed if you see small cracks such as these. If, on the other hand, you see large cracks running down the wall, you can almost bet the house has a foundation problem.

If the house was not built on a slab, but was built with a basement foundation instead, you must be particularly aware of moisture problems. This is fairly common, especially in older homes. Look for cracks in the basement walls that may have evidence of leaking around them, such as staining or mildew. Leaks in the walls can also create a buildup of mold in the basement area, an issue that is becoming a major liability for some homeowners. It is not at all unusual to observe hairline cracks in the basement floor or even in the walls. In fact, I don't believe I've ever seen one without some kind of small cracks. You don't need to be overly concerned about these types of cracks, as they are usually just surface cracks that do not go all the way through the floor or the wall. Any house with foundation problems can be very costly to repair, whether built on slabs or on basements. As a general rule, your best bet is to avoid houses with these types of issues.

Roofs are another area that may require major repairs. The cost to repair a roof can vary widely with age and condition. Most composition shingles have a minimum life of 25 years, so if the existing shingles are less than 15 years old, it's a pretty safe bet that repairs will be minimal. After 15 years, the shingles can begin curling up and wearing to the point where leaks may begin to develop. Newer roofs can show signs of discoloration, but this is a problem that can be easily and inexpensively resolved by applying a chemical cleaning process. The discoloration is usually caused by a buildup of mildew, which can be killed and removed with a solution of water and bleach (available at most hardware stores). If a new roof is needed, the cost to replace it may not be prohibitive. If, for example, a new layer of shingles can be applied over the existing layer, the cost and time involved is minimal. On the other hand, if two or three layers of shingles already exist, then a teardown will almost certainly be necessary. This can effectively double the price of a new roof, as the labor required for the teardown can be quite expensive due to the additional time that is needed. Furthermore, older homes with several layers of existing shingles may require additional work. The roof deck may be damaged as a result of water leaks that have occurred over time. If the house needs to be completely redecked, this will certainly drive up the cost.

Other repairs that may prove costly include replacing equipment, windows, and exterior surfaces such as brick or siding. If the furnace and air conditioner are worn out, replacing them can quickly add up. New windows for the entire house can also be quite expensive. Replacing the siding or brick on a house can add thousands of dollars to the cost of your repairs. A close inspection of these items is essential for the success of your project. It may be that only minor repairs are needed, that only one or two windows need to be replaced, or that the exterior of the house just needs a fresh coat of paint. These types of improvements are easy to make, do not require much time, and most of all, do not require as much money as major repairs.

The house's plumbing should also be carefully checked for proper operation. The plumbing can be checked by flushing toilets, inspecting underneath sink cabinets, and looking for leaky faucets. You will also want to check the age and condition of the home's hot water heater. Leaky faucets and hot water heaters are fairly easy to repair and/or replace and can be done quickly and inexpensively. With homes older than 20 years, you will want to make a special note to determine if the roots from mature plants or trees are causing any blockage. Recurring problems in the same line are usually symptomatic of root damage. Some older sewage lines are made of a claylike material, and the roots of nearby trees can literally grow right through the sewer lines. When that happens, it creates a blockage within the line and causes the sewer system to back up. I bought a house a number of years ago that was 40 years old or so, which I then rented out. Sure enough, I had one line in particular that kept getting backed up. It cost me $75 every time the plumber came out to clear the line. As it turned out, the line was severely blocked with roots that had grown through it. I finally had the plumber dig up the backyard line, which was made of clay, and replace it with a new PVC line.

Sewer lines that run through a concrete slab foundation or through concrete driveways can get backed up as a result of settling. As the concrete settles, the sewer lines, which are usually

PVC, will crack and break. The separation in the line does not allow the sewage to drain properly and can also cause the line to back up. In another house I bought, the driveway had a large crack in it due to settling. When I purchased the house, I wasn't really too concerned about the crack because initially I thought I would just patch the driveway with a little cement. As it turns out, the repair was much more costly. The concrete driveway had to be chiseled out with a jackhammer to replace the broken sewage line. Once the line was repaired, a new driveway had to be poured. As an investor, you will want to minimize dealing with the more severe types of plumbing problems such as these. Leaky faucets and hot water heaters are generally easy to repair or replace. Broken sewer lines, on the other hand, are harder to detect and can be much more expensive to repair. A careful inspection of the plumbing system can potentially save you thousands of dollars.

Finally, the home's electrical wiring should be checked for proper working condition. A simple check of outlets and light switches can tell you a great deal about a house's electrical condition. If they are working properly, chances are the system is okay. Homes older than 30 to 40 years tend to have more problems, as breakers and switches may eventually wear out. In some homes, the wiring may be so old that it will have to be completely replaced. Installing an entirely new electrical system can be very expensive, due in part to the fact that much of the wiring runs behind the walls of a house. The new wiring will either have to be fished or pulled through openings from the attic or basement, if there are any, or cuts will have to be made in the drywall, which will then have to be repaired and repainted.

As you gain more experience and look at more and more properties, you will be able to quickly assess a house's physical condition and know within a short time whether it meets your investment criteria. If you lack experience or are not yet comfortable with the inspection process, you may want to hire a professional house inspection company. These companies perform a very thorough inspection and give you a written report when they are finished. Their services commonly cost anywhere between $150 and $500, depending on the area of the country you live in and the size of the house. I seldom use professional inspectors anymore because, more often than not, they end up telling me what I already knew from my own inspection. About the only time I do use them is if the house is well beyond the 30-year age mark. In fact, just recently I had an inspection performed on a house I had under contract that was built in 1903. The main reason I wanted an inspection in this particular case was to ensure that the wiring was up to current code. As previously mentioned, replacing the entire wiring in a house can be very expensive. As it turned out, the electrical wiring did in fact meet current code requirements. The $335 I spent on the inspection was well worth it to me.

In summary, the ideal property will look as though it's in a lot worse shape than it actually is. You should focus your efforts on finding houses that are in relatively good condition, but that look like dumps. This is difficult for many people to do, and that is exactly why an astute investor such as yourself can profit handsomely from the retailing business. It's hard to look beyond that first impression of a house, especially if it's a negative one. Most people will keep right on driving. They won't even stop to look at such a house! They absolutely cannot see the hidden potential just waiting to be unlocked in properties like these. As an investor who is serious about flipping properties, you *must* be able to look beyond what you see on the surface. In fact, you will come to enjoy driving up to a house that appears to be run down and lacking in care, because experience has taught you that these houses are actually diamonds in the rough. While most people see a lump of coal, you will come to recognize it as a diamond that just needs a little polishing. Ideally, you will be able to buy houses at coal-like prices and sell these highly polished gems at diamond-like prices.

This same concept can be applied on a larger scale. For example, I have used it in the apartment business as well as in the residential home construction business. As a principal in Symphony

Homes, I recently took over an entire community that was partially completed with new homes and successfully applied the value play strategy. The community was only about three years old, but the original builder there apparently ran into financial difficulties that caused the progress of new home construction to come to a standstill. As a result, the entranceway and all of the remaining vacant lots became neglected. Weeds and grass went uncut and grew as high as four to five feet. Many of the vacant lots were littered with debris left over from the previous builder. In short, the community was a real eyesore! The developer of the subdivision had tried unsuccessfully for over six months to get another builder to come in and take over where the previous builder had left off. No one would touch it. In fact, you would probably be considered foolish to go in and take over something like that. Discussions with the city inspectors led me to believe that even they had written off this project.

However, experience has taught me to look beyond what is visible on the surface. Let's take a closer look at the facts of this particular community.

First we'll look at the negatives:

■ The entrance into the community was overgrown with weeds.
■ The weeds were overgrown on all of the vacant lots.
■ Many of the lots were littered with debris left over from the previous builder.
■ The residents and city officials were in despair and had given up hope.

Now let's look at the positives:

■ Landscaping improvements to the entrance would be quick and easy to make.
■ Weeds can be easily cut, and this is an inexpensive and quick way to improve a property's appearance.

- Debris is easy to remove.
- The community was ideally situated immediately off of a main road that provided terrific visibility to passersby.
- A brand-new post office was located directly across the street, which meant that no less than once or twice a month, everyone in town would drive by the community and see the improvements being made along with all the new construction activity.
- The community was located only one-half mile from a major state road that was heavily traveled and only a mile or so from a major interstate highway. Both of these roads served as major traffic arteries for commuters and would be easily accessible from the community.
- The homes in the community were only three years old or less, which meant that our new homes would fit in perfectly.

As it turned out, our company was able to negotiate a very favorable price and subsequently took over the remaining lots. As a condition for doing so, the developer agreed at his expense to have all of the vacant lots mowed, the debris removed, and the entranceway cleaned up immediately upon closing. Within one week, the community was cleaned up and a sense of pride was restored to the residents who lived there. In fact, the existing residents in the community treated us like knights in shining armor who had come to their rescue. They were thankful that finally another builder had taken enough interest in their community to come in and make a positive difference. Their sincere expression of gratitude toward us meant a great deal and was certainly appreciated by the Symphony Homes team. Our ability to envision the hidden potential in that community has allowed us to enjoy a substantially higher profit margin on a per-unit basis than we otherwise would have.

In summary, don't underestimate the power of the value play strategy. It is indisputably one of the most effective means available to you to create wealth and to enjoy a fuller and more reward-ing life.

> I believe life is constantly testing us for our level of commitment, and life's greatest rewards are reserved for those who demonstrate a never-ending commit-ment to act until they achieve. This level of resolve can move mountains, but it must be constant and con-sistent. As simplistic as this may sound, it is still the common denominator separating those who live their dreams from those who live in regret.
> —*Anthony Robbins*

Chapter 4

Ten Ways to Locate Properties

$\mathbb{F}$inding exactly the right property can sometimes prove to be challenging. The application of a comprehensive and all-inclusive approach will provide you with the greatest chances for success. You must be willing to exercise patience and diligence in your search. Doing so will enable you to minimize your risk and maximize the return of your hard-earned investment capital. The more selection options you have available to you, the better your odds for locating the type of property most suited to your objectives. In my experience, brokers, classified ads, real estate publications, web sites, real estate investment clubs, and lenders have all proven to be useful at one time or another. Advertising, for sale by owners, vacant properties, and foreclosures can also generate good leads. (See Exhibit 4.1.)

REAL ESTATE AGENTS

Having several real estate agents scouting properties for you is one of the most effective ways to quickly and efficiently identify potential properties that can be flipped. I must stress that it is *critical to your success* to ensure the competency level of the brokerage team you put together. I have worked with many brokers and agents whose range of expertise and experience varies greatly.

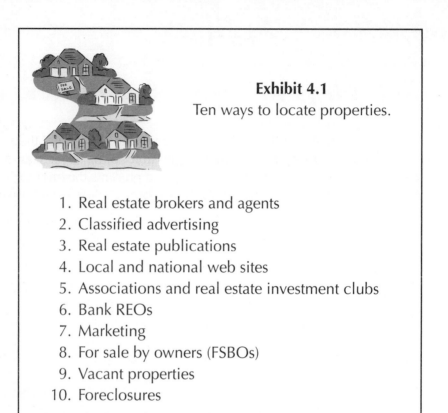

Exhibit 4.1
Ten ways to locate properties.

1. Real estate brokers and agents
2. Classified advertising
3. Real estate publications
4. Local and national web sites
5. Associations and real estate investment clubs
6. Bank REOs
7. Marketing
8. For sale by owners (FSBOs)
9. Vacant properties
10. Foreclosures

Most residential brokers focus primarily on the more traditional single-family-housing sales. They act in a fiduciary capacity to represent buyers and sellers who have a broad and diverse range of needs. The sales process typically goes something like this:

SALES AGENT: Mr. Buyer, what type of home are you looking for?

BUYER: We're looking for a three-bedroom, two-bath ranch.

SALES AGENT: Great! Have you been prequalified?

BUYER: Yes, Ms. Agent. Our loan officer has preapproved us for $150,000.

SALES AGENT: That's terrific, Mr. Buyer! What area of town do you prefer?

BUYER: I work on the north side of town, so something within 15 minutes or so would be ideal.

SALES AGENT: That's wonderful! The MLS shows there are 12 homes available in the area you prefer and 8 of them are within your price range!

The sales agent will then schedule time with the buyer and the sellers to visit as many of the homes as possible. If the buyer sees something he likes, the agent writes it up and presents the offer to the seller. There is often a counteroffer or two before a deal is consummated. The broker collects her commission on closing and the buyer lives happily ever after . . . well, maybe.

While this is a simplified example of how the sales process works, the process for locating properties that can be flipped does share a few similarities with the more traditional role the sales agent plays. The sales agent will locate the types of properties you are looking for, present them to you, and if an opportunity makes financial sense, you will make an offer for the agent to present to the seller. Significant information that traditional sales agents are *not* used to providing is data specific to the market you are buying in. If requested, they may provide a few comparables, or *comps* as they are known, but you need lots of hard data that will support your investment decision. Housing prices vary widely from city to city and from community to community. Prices are relative. For example, an identical house selling for $85,000 in one neighborhood might be worth $110,000 in another neighborhood. That's a difference of $25,000 for two identical houses. You must have market data that will enable you to make sound investment decisions.

In addition to traditional real estate sales agent, there are agents who specialize in investment properties and nothing else. These are the dealers we discussed in Chapter 2. These are the people you want on your team! Dealers play an important role in bringing opportunities to investors. They often act as wholesalers for retailers and other investors looking to buy property at below-market prices. Dealers are oftentimes licensed real estate agents and earn their money from commissions generated. These agents are generally experts in their industry who have migrated from single-family residential sales for one reason or another—usually because of a shared interest they have for investment properties. Their specialized knowledge can save you a great deal in time, energy, and money. While traditional sales agents are not used to providing their clients with market data, dealers know exactly what you need. They understand the nature of the business of flipping properties and recognize that you will need key market information for proper financial analysis.

Dealers are well informed and are in direct contact with buyers and sellers every single day. They know which areas of town are hot and which are not. They also know when new properties are about to be made available for sale, so if they know what you are looking for, they can notify you immediately when a property meeting your criteria hits the market. Since dealers are plugged into a network of relationships—people who provide them with information and inventory—they will be among the first to know when a new opportunity becomes available. An additional advantage dealers can offer is that they often have an extensive database of other investors, both buyers and sellers, whom they can contact. Even if a house is not officially listed for sale, the broker may know from a prior conversation that the owner would entertain an offer should the right buyer come along with the right price.

Furthermore, dealers will often know how to use the MLS in ways that traditional real estate agents may not be aware of. For example, they can search the description fields of homes available for sale for keywords like "handyman special" or "TLC needed." Other keywords include "needs work," "as is," and "seller motivated." One additional term your dealer can search for is "VLB," which means "vacant on lock box." This frequently indicates that the seller has already moved into another house for any number of reasons (transfer, new home, etc.) and is now in the unenviable position of making two house payments. The house is likely to be in fairly good condition, with only minimal repairs needed, but a seller making two house payments may be willing to take considerably less than the true market value. I found myself in that very position several years ago. My wife and I bought a new house in Michigan and were required to close on it even though we had not yet sold our home in Texas. After about six months of making payments on both houses, a buyer offered me much less than similar houses in the neighborhood were selling for. I wasn't at all excited about taking less than I thought the house was worth, but I was thankful for the opportunity to be relieved of the mortgage obligation on the other residence. Meanwhile, the buyer got a great deal, and I am certain he could sell the house today for much more than he paid for it.

CLASSIFIED ADVERTISING

Almost all newspapers, large or small, carry a section in their classified advertising specifically for selling real estate. Many of these ads are placed by real estate agents and are designed to prompt you to call their office. Most homes listed for sale in the newspaper by agents are active listings and will typically be priced at full retail. You might notice some ads, however, that use keywords like "motivated seller" or "must sell, owner transferring." These types of classified advertisements are worth following up on. Even if the home is no longer available or it does not meet your investment objectives, it can provide you with an opportunity to create a dialogue with a sales agent who might be able to find investment property that will meet your needs. The agent may even refer you to someone in his or her office who specializes in investment property (e.g., a dealer).

Many of the ads listed in the classified section are for sale by owners (FSBOs). Again, you will want to look for any keywords that may indicate the owner is anxious to sell or that the property may be offered at a price below retail. Some of these keywords include "handyman special," "needs work," or "as is." You should be prepared to take the time to call on as many of these property owners as possible. You must also have the self-discipline to exercise restraint in your selection and analysis process. It is easy to get excited about an opportunity and to become emotionally engaged in the buying process. To be successful, you have to be able to remain impartial and objective in your analysis. Sooner or later, your patience will pay off and you will find that diamond in the rough.

Another way to use the classified advertising section is to place your own ad in the real estate wanted section. You don't need to spend a lot of money on these ads. A well-written small ad can be just as effective as a larger and more expensive ad. Your goal is to motivate people who want to sell their house to call you. Your ad should be designed to solicit only those callers who are likely to be selling the type of property that you are seeking. Following are some sample ads you may want to consider using.

NEED QUICK CASH?
I BUY HOUSES!
FAST CLOSINGS! ALL CASH!
CALL (800) 123-4567

MOTIVATED SELLERS WANTED!
ANY CONDITION! FAST CLOSINGS!
WE BUY HOUSES!
CALL (800) 123-4567

VACANT AND HANDYMAN SPECIAL
PROPERTIES WANTED!
ANY AREA! ANY CONDITION!
(800) 123-4567

REAL ESTATE PUBLICATIONS

Almost all areas periodically publish books or magazines specifically designed for residential real estate sales. Some of these are local, while others are regional. The magazines can often be found in racks or newsstands located outside real estate offices, convenience stores, and grocery stores. These real estate publications can be a very good source for locating potential deals. You will also find many helpful real estate–related advertisers in these publications—real estate agents, mortgage companies, appraisers, surveyors, title companies, real estate legal services, and insurance companies.

The majority of ads in these magazines are placed by real estate agents who tend to place all of their listings on one page. The ads usually feature a photo of the agent along with some compelling reason why you should contact that person for your real estate needs. Although the bulk of the ads in real estate magazines are placed by agents and brokers, some do offer an FSBO section. While most of the sales agents with listings in these publications focus on the traditional retail housing segment, there are usually a number of agents who specialize in different niches within the real estate market. For example, some firms focus solely on commercial real estate, while others specialize in vacant land. Still others (e.g., dealers) specialize in the wholesale market. As discussed in Chapter 2, dealers can be an excellent source for you. A good dealer can fax 20 or 30 wholesale listings to your office within minutes of receiving your call. Don't overlook these easy-to-find real estate publications, as they can provide you with lots of leads and lots of information vital to your success!

LOCAL AND NATIONAL WEB SITES

A number of web sites offer all kinds of information about houses for sale. You can do a local search by keying in a phrase such as "homes for sale Dallas, TX," for example. A search like this will usually generate results of 20 to 30, maybe even more, web sites with listings in your area. The most comprehensive and well-known web site related to single-family properties for sale is hosted by the National Association of Realtors. You can find it at www.realtor.com. Realtor.com boasts over 2 million listings for various types of properties, including single-family homes, condominiums, town houses, multifamily apartments, mobile homes, vacant land, farms, and rentals. The data derived for these listings comes from the Multiple Listing Service, so it will not include any properties for sale by owner. The web site is available to the general public, so you don't have to be a real estate agent to access its listings. It is very much like a public MLS for properties available to the general population—or at least anyone with a computer and access to the web. You can also search by property type, state, city, zip code, price range, minimum and maximum square feet, age of home, number of floors, and several other criteria. Most listings provide a descriptive overview of the property, photos, and offering information. Exhibit 4.2 illustrates how very specific you can be by using the search criteria available at Realtor.com.

Other good Internet sources include your local newspapers. Almost all major newspapers now list their entire classified section on web sites. The information is often updated daily. This is usually determined by how often the paper is published. For example, a daily paper is most likely to be updated daily. A weekly paper would be updated weekly. An advantage the newspaper web sites offer over a site such as Realtor.com is that in addition to providing ads placed by real estate agents, many ads are also placed by individuals or owners. In fact, other than placing a sign out in the front yard, this is really about the only way an individual can market his or her property. Newspaper classifieds are not nearly as comprehensive as a site like Realtor.com, but they do provide you with a good mix of properties for sale by both real estate agents and individual homeowners.

These are only two of many web sites that can help you locate investment opportunities. The best way to locate properties in

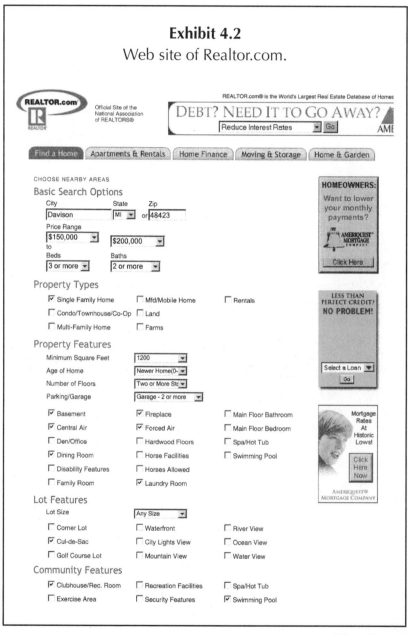

Exhibit 4.2
Web site of Realtor.com.

(Continues)

Exhibit 4.2
(Continued)

☐ Golf   ☐ Senior Community   ☑ Tennis

FREE MATERIAL LIST FOR YOUR DREAM HOME

Financial Options

☐ Lease Option Considered

☐ Trade Considered

MLS ID Search

MLS ID

(You'll need to fill in the City and State fields at the top of the page to complete an MLS search.)

Show Properties

Site Map | Corporate News & Info | Contact Us | Advertise With Us | Join our staff
Terms of Use and Privacy Policy.

© 1995-2002 NATIONAL ASSOCIATION OF REALTORS® and Homestore, Inc. All rights reserved. Equal Housing Opportunity
REALTOR.com® is the official site of the National Association of REALTORS® and is operated by Homestore, Inc.

REALTOR® -- A registered collective membership mark that identifies a real estate professional who is a member of the National Association of REALT subscribes to its strict Code of Ethics. Inquiries regarding the Code of Ethics should be directed to the board in which a REALTOR® holds member

---

your own area is to use a search engine like Yahoo, Google, or MSN to do a specific search.

REAL ESTATE INVESTMENT CLUBS

Most cities have a number of real estate investment–related associations and clubs. These clubs provide an excellent opportunity for you to network with others who share similar interests. Members often include investors like yourself, real estate brokers, tax and real estate attorneys, architectural engineers, appraisers, and other real estate professionals. Clubs and associations usually meet on a periodic basis, such as monthly, to discuss current events and share information. In addition, they frequently feature guest speakers who provide insight into a given area of expertise. You can find real estate associations in your area by looking in the yellow pages or by doing a search on the Internet. One site that I have used is called Real Estate Promo.com and is located at www.realestatepromo.com. Click on the link titled "Investment Clubs" to locate a club near you. Clubs listed include almost all 50 states, so you should be able to find something near you. A similar site is offered by a company called Creative Real Estate Online, located at www.real-estate-online.com. Go to the home page and click on "Real Estate Clubs" to find an investment association in your area.

BANK REOs

Smaller local or regional banks can also be a good source for locating properties. Lenders are not in the business of managing real estate, nor do they want to be. The very nature of their business, however, demands that they assume risk with each and every loan extended to borrowers. Unfortunately for the banks, sometimes those borrowers default. When they do, the lender forecloses on the property and the real estate is transferred into the lender's real estate owned (REO) portfolio.

Most people don't event know that REOs exist. Banks certainly don't promote the fact that they've had to foreclose on real estate, which is now listed on their books as a nonperforming loan. After all, their customers come to them for banking services, not real estate services. Although almost all banks have REOs, very few will publicize that information. Small local banks usually have one individual who is responsible for the real estate owned portfolio, while regional banks may have several people, or even a whole department, responsible for REOs. Banks divest these properties through a network of private investors who have expressed an interest in them and also through real estate agents (e.g., dealers who specialize in wholesale property). The network of private investors can include anyone. If you are interested in acquiring properties in this manner, then you will need to be prepared to do some initial legwork to establish the proper contacts. There is no limit to the number of banks you can contact. I recommend establishing relationships with 8 to 10 banks in your area to provide you with a large of a pool of houses for sale.

Lenders are often quite flexible in the terms and conditions they are willing to offer, which may result in an opportunity for you to reach an agreement that is acceptable to both of you. The basis for the lender's initial asking price will likely be determined by the hard costs the bank has put into it, or its book value. While the bank will no doubt make every effort to minimize its losses, if it is anxious to get the property off its books, there's a good chance it will be willing to negotiate in your favor by agreeing to write down a portion of the loan. You should take time to physically inspect the property, then determine the costs required for repairs, the carrying costs, and the transaction costs and make your offer to the bank based on your analysis. In other words, determine the maximum amount you can invest in the deal and still make money based on a rate of return that is acceptable to you. If the deal doesn't make sense for you as an investor, you're better off letting the bank keep it. After all, there are many more banks with just as many REO properties available that may meet your investment criteria.

MARKETING

As you graduate from buying and selling real estate on a part-time basis to a full-time business, you will want to give serious consideration to promoting your company and the services you offer. Just as other business owners budget a certain portion of their expected revenues for marketing purposes, so will you, too, want to allocate a portion of your resources to promoting your real estate investment company. The more people who know that you are in business to buy and sell houses, the more opportunities you will have presented to you.

There are numerous ways to market your business and just as many books written about how to do so. Since this is not a marketing book, I will mention just a few of the many ways you can promote your company. Some of these include advertising in newspapers and magazines, implementing a direct mail campaign, using signs, and doing a broadcast fax.

As previously mentioned, you can place small ads in the classified section of the newspaper, which can be highly effective. As your company grows, however, you will want to consider placing larger display ads in newspapers and in real estate publications. You can advertise in the same newspapers and magazines that you use to search for properties to buy. It should be easy enough for you to make your ad stand out from all of the others because you are in the business of buying houses at wholesale, while most all of the other advertisers are buying and selling houses at retail. The sample ad shown in Exhibit 4.3 is just one of many ideas you can use to promote your company. The focus of this ad is to generate referrals by offering a $500 reward for each and every referral received. You should be sure to qualify your offer, however, by stating that the referral must result in the signing of a purchase agreement by both the buyer and the seller.

Another very effective method of promoting your company is to implement a direct mail campaign. Since the cost of printing and postage can quickly add up, your direct mail piece should be targeted to the people who can best help you—real estate agents. You can purchase a list of names and addresses for the agents in your area from a reputable company, or, if you have the time, simply use your local telephone book to build your own list. Much of the content used in your display ads in newspapers and real estate publications can also be used in your direct mail piece. The literature mailed can be in the form of a letter that introduces you and the services you offer, a flyer containing the same information, a sales brochure, or any combination of the three. I suggest that you also include at least two to three of your business cards. While the recipients of your mailing may discard the enclosed letter or flyer, they will most likely save your business cards, and if you include more than one, there's a good chance they may pass one along to a business associate.

Signs are a cost-effective way of marketing your company. Smaller signs, perhaps 18 by 24 inches and made out of corrugated plastic, are fairly inexpensive to buy. You can buy them with wire-

Exhibit 4.3
Example of a promotional ad.

frame stands, which makes them easy to place in high-traffic locations. I recommend not putting too much information on your signs. Just stick to the basics, such as "I buy houses," your company name, and a telephone number. I've seen some real estate signs that are so overloaded with information that it's difficult to make out anything, especially when people are driving by and may have only a few seconds to glance at the sign. Use large letters and keep your sign simple. I would also suggest using a color that works well in both winter and summer. For example, white signs with blue lettering look great in the summer; however, in the winter the white sign will blend in with the snow and barely be visible. Likewise, a green sign with white lettering looks great in the wintertime because the colors are sharply contrasting. Once again, though, in the summer the green sign blends in with grassy roadsides and surrounding foliage. I suggest using colors that work well year-round, such as a red or blue sign with white letters.

As your company grows and you have more available in your advertising budget, you may also want to consider using billboards. These signs can be very effective, especially in areas of town where the traffic count is known to be high. It is also helpful if the posted speed limit is 40 miles per hour or less. That way, the passersby have more time to read the information on the signs. As with the smaller roadside signs, don't try to put too much information on billboards. Drivers usually have only a couple of seconds to read your message. Again, keep it simple.

Finally, you may want to consider faxing your message to as many recipients as possible. Your primary target market should be real estate offices. A number of good fax programs allow you to generate what is known as a *broadcast fax* directly from your computer. These programs are easy to use and easy to set up. A broadcast fax, also known as a *blast fax,* allows you to send a document via facsimile to multiple recipients. The fax program allows you to set up telephone directories. For example, you could set up a directory named Genesee County Real Estate and enter the fax numbers of 100 real estate agents. When you get ready to send your letter, flyer, or other document from your computer, the fax program allows you to select the entire directory. All you do is click on it, hit Send, and the program will do the rest. It will spend the next two to three hours dialing every number in your directory and sending the fax. If you live in an area where the calls are all local, then the faxes cost you only a little bit of your time. One cautionary note I will add is that many people do not want to receive faxes they consider to be advertisements. As a general rule, the real estate community will be receptive to your message; however, be respectful of those who do not wish to receive faxes and promptly remove them from your list.

FOR SALE BY OWNERS (FSBOs)

Individuals who prefer to sell their own houses are frequently referred to as *for sale by owners,* or FSBOs. This group of homeowners represents an important segment of the potential properties available to you, so be sure to give them the attention they deserve. They can be located by looking through the classified section of your local newspaper or by driving through neighborhoods and looking for FSBO signs. FSBOs typically maintain the attitude that they can sell their houses on their own without any professional help from the real estate community, thereby enabling them to save thousands of dollars on the cost of the commission. What they fail to realize, unfortunately, is that although they may save money on the commission, they may lose more money on the overall transaction than if they had listed with an agent. This results from their lack of experience and lack of knowledge of local market prices.

FSBOs all have an idea of how much they think their houses are worth, but in reality, their houses are usually priced too high or too low. For example, some owners have lived in their homes for 20 years or more and have no idea how much homes have appreciated during that time. Another homeowner may have heard that a neighbor down the street sold her house for $X;$ therefore his house must be worth $Y.$ In truth, neither seller really knows the true market value of their home. Guess what? That's good news for you as an investor. Since you will be intimately familiar with market values in the neighborhoods you will be prospecting, you will know immediately from your initial telephone conversation with a potential seller whether the price of the house fits your investment criteria. If you find a seller who is willing to sell his or her home at a price 10 or 15 percent below market, that can certainly work to your advantage. For those of you who may think this is taking advantage of the seller, I disagree. You have no moral obligation to tell sellers that their house may be worth more than they are asking. FSBOs set their asking price at a value they believe to be fair for any number of reasons. As a buyer willing to meet their terms, you have become an important component of a relationship that is amenable to both parties. Finally, for sale by owners are often flexible on terms and may be able to provide you with a more favorable and creative deal structure, one that permits you to minimize your cash outlay in the property.

VACANT PROPERTIES

As you drive through neighborhoods in your search for investment opportunities, be sure to pay special attention to those houses that appear vacant. Vacant houses are more of a liability than an asset for their owners, so they are oftentimes available at bargain prices. For any number of reasons, the seller has moved out and is no longer around to care for the house. It may be that he or she just went through a divorce, had a new house built, or was transferred to another area. Whatever the reason, the end result is the same. If the owner is to prevent the house from going into foreclosure, he or she must not only make the payments on the new house, but must also keep up the payments on the old one. After just a few months of making double house payments, sellers of vacant properties become very motivated. In some cases, they are happy just to have somebody relieve them of their monthly obligation, regardless of any equity they may have built up in the house.

Obvious signs of empty houses include overgrown weeds and shrubs, newspapers in the driveway, and a general rundown appearance. Sometimes these houses have only recently been vacated; other times they have been sitting empty for several months. They may have an FSBO sign or a real estate firm's sign in the front yard. If so, this makes your job of finding the owner much easier. If there is no sign out front, you may have to do a little research. Usually, a telephone call to the local taxing authority can provide you with the information you need. The clerks who work in the tax offices and who are responsible for maintaining the tax roles can quickly and easily provide you with the current owner's name and the address (to which the tax bill is mailed). With the name and address, you can call information to obtain a phone number for the owner. If the number is unlisted, you can express your interest in the property through the mail since you at least have the owner's address. Be sure and provide owners with your telephone number so that if they are interested in selling, they can contact you with as little effort as possible.

FORECLOSURES

While vacant properties can be an excellent source of finding investment opportunities, properties that sit vacant for too long often become foreclosed properties. This, too, can be another great source for finding potential deals. Buying and selling foreclosures requires an individual to have a working knowledge of that market. While a number of good books have been written on the subject, many investors do not have the expertise or the time to find undervalued foreclosures. Furthermore, they are unfamiliar with the auction and/or bidding process and may lack the resources to purchase properties in this manner. An investor who understands the process of buying foreclosed properties can potentially make substantial profits. Buying foreclosures, however, is not as easy as many would have you believe. In many markets, the bidding process is very competitive and therefore the property is difficult to buy at an attractive price. The investor participating in this market must have specialized knowledge, patience, and enough investment capital to be successful.

The best approach to identifying the property best suited to your specific needs will include using as many of these tools as possible. The most important thing to remember is to *be patient.* You will find the right property at the right price with the right terms. As the employer of your capital, your task is to have your employees (your capital) working as hard for you as possible. That means your investment must offer an acceptable rate of return to you. Only you can determine what is acceptable. It is best to establish an acceptable rate of return early in the process so you don't make the mistake of lowering your standards because you think you have found a property that is okay. Determine your investment criteria and objectives, implement them as an initial filtering device, and when the time comes, be prepared to execute your acquisition strategy.

> **The heights by great men reached and kept,**
> **Were not attained by sudden flight,**
> **But they, while their companions slept,**
> **Were toiling upward in the night.**
> *—Henry Wadsworth Longfellow*

Chapter 5

Valuation Methodologies

Now that you understand the concept of flipping properties, how to create value, and what types of properties to look for, the next step is to learn how to analyze potential value play opportunities to determine whether they meet your investment criteria. This chapter is probably the most critical chapter in the entire book. The key to your success in buying and selling single-family houses is to have a thorough and comprehensive understanding of value. Proper valuation is the basis for all investment decisions, whether they be investments in the stocks of various companies, in commodities, or in real estate. You absolutely must be able to understand how value is derived in order to make rational and balanced investment decisions. Without these essential skill sets, you will find yourself at a tremendous disadvantage.

Before you even make an offer on a prospective investment property, you will want to know beforehand the potential value that can be created from it. Creating value in single-family houses can be accomplished in several ways. Your review of a prospective flipping opportunity will consist of examining the variable components of the property that affect its value—in other words, anything at all about the property that can be changed to add value. For flipping or rehab properties, this would primarily include, for example, the physical condition of the property, but not its location. While the property's location is certainly important, it is not a variable that can be changed to add value.

HOW TO KNOW HOW MUCH IS TOO MUCH

In this chapter, you learn how to determine whether a house priced at $50,000 is in fact worth the seller's asking price. How do you know? It may in reality be worth only $40,000, or it could actually be underpriced and may be worth $65,000. The bottom line is you need to know and understand the difference for yourself and not rely solely on what the sales agent and/or seller is telling you. In my experience, I have seen many agents who believe their client's property is worth more than it really is. I have also seen inexperienced investors attempt to justify the value imbued in the price the agent is asking. Somehow they think if they could only buy the property, they are going to be able to unlock all that extra value that really doesn't exist. The truth is, however, they will have overpaid for the property. Paying too much for a rehab property is the quickest way I know to put you out of business.

VALUATION METHODOLOGIES

Three traditional approaches are used to determine the value of a property: the *sales comparison approach,* the *cost approach,* and the *income capitalization approach.* (See Exhibit 5.1.) Each approach has its place and serves a unique function in determining value. Depending on the type of property being appraised, the majority of the weight may be given to a particular approach, as the other two methods may not be relevant.

Replacement Cost Approach

In an appraisal report conducted by Butler Burgher, Inc., a well-known appraisal firm based in Houston, Texas, the replacement cost approach is defined as follows:

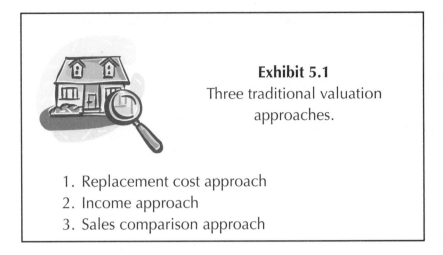

Exhibit 5.1
Three traditional valuation
approaches.

1. Replacement cost approach
2. Income approach
3. Sales comparison approach

The cost approach is based on the premise that the value of a property can be indicated by the current cost to construct a reproduction or replacement for the improvements minus the amount of depreciation evident in the structures from all causes plus the value of the land and entrepreneurial profit. This approach to value is particularly useful for appraising new or nearly new improvements.

The replacement cost approach is usually not used to value investment properties such as single-family houses. It is most appropriately used when estimating the actual costs associated with replacing all of the physical assets. For example, if a house was partially or completely destroyed by fire, the value established from the cost approach would be useful in helping to determine exactly how much an insurance company would pay for the resulting damages. Depending on the type of policy you have in place, the insurance company may only pay for the remaining useful life of the item damaged. For example, if the roof on the house is 20 years old and is damaged as a result of high winds, the insurance company may not pay 100 percent of the cost for a brand-new roof. If the estimated life of the shingles is 25 years, insurance may only reimburse you for the remaining useful life, which in this case would be 20 percent.

$$\text{Remaining useful life} = 1 - \frac{20}{25} = 20\%$$

When buying insurance for your investment properties, be sure to determine exactly what your policy covers and what it does not cover.

Income Capitalization Approach

I again refer to the appraisal firm of Butler Burgher to define the income capitalization approach, or income approach, as it is also known.

> The income capitalization approach is based on the principle of anticipation which recognizes the present value of the future income benefits to be derived from ownership of real property. The income approach is most applicable to properties that are considered for investment purposes, and is considered very reliable when adequate income/expense data are available. Since income producing real estate is most often purchased by investors, this approach is valid and is generally considered the most applicable.
>
> The income capitalization approach is a process of estimating the value of real property based upon the principle that value is directly related to the present value of all future net income attributable to the property. The value of the real property is therefore derived by capitalizing net income either by direct capitalization or a discounted cash flow analysis. Regardless of the capitalization technique employed, one must attempt to estimate a reasonable net operating income based upon the

best available market data. The derivation of this estimate requires the appraiser to 1) project potential gross
income (PGI) based upon an analysis of the subject rent
roll and a comparison of the subject to competing properties, 2) project income loss from vacancy and collec-
tions based on the subject's occupancy history and upon
supply and demand relationships in the subject's market . . . , 3) derive effective gross income (EGI) by subtracting the vacancy and collection income loss from
PGI, 4) project the operating expenses associated with
the production of the income stream by analysis of the
subject's operating history and comparison of the subject to similar competing properties, and 5) derive net
operating income (NOI) by subtracting the operating
expenses from EGI.

The preceding technical description by Butler Burgher defining the income approach may initially appear somewhat complex
to those of you who may not be familiar with the methodologies
used for the analysis of financial statements. The income
approach can be broken down to its most basic and fundamental
level by examining a simple financial instrument such as a certificate of deposit. For example, assuming a market interest rate of
5 percent, how much would you be willing to pay for an annuity
yielding $10,000 per annum? The answer is easily solved by tak-
ing a simple ratio of the two values as follows:

$$\text{Present value} = \frac{\text{income}}{\text{rate}} = \frac{\$10,000}{0.05} = \$200,000$$

In other words, if you purchased a certificate of deposit for
$200,000 that yielded 5 percent annually, you could expect an
income stream of $10,000. It doesn't matter how long the income
continues. The present value remains the same and will continue
to generate an income stream of $10,000 as long as you continue
to hold the $200,000 certificate of deposit. If at some point in

your real estate career you decide to invest in income-producing properties such as apartments, strip centers, or office buildings, I urge you to thoroughly acquaint yourself with the income capitalization approach and to become proficient in its application. In *The Complete Guide to Buying and Selling Apartment Buildings,* I expound on these principles in depth and provide many examples of this particular valuation approach.

Sales Comparison Approach

Once again, I rely on Butler Burgher to define the third valuation approach, which is the sales comparison approach:

> The sales comparison approach is founded upon the principle of substitution which holds that the cost to acquire an equally desirable substitute property without undue delay ordinarily sets the upper limit of value. At any given time, prices paid for comparable properties are construed by many to reflect the value of the property appraised. The validity of a value indication derived by this approach is heavily dependent upon the availability of data on recent sales of properties similar in location, size, and utility to the appraised property.
>
> The sales comparison approach is premised upon the principle of substitution—a valuation principle that states that a prudent purchaser would pay no more for real property than the cost of acquiring an equally desirable substitute on the open market. The principle of substitution presumes that the purchaser will consider the alternatives available to them, that they will act rationally or prudently on the basis of his information about those alternatives, and that time is not a significant factor. Substitution may assume the form of the purchase of an existing property with the same utility, or of acquiring an investment which will produce an income stream of the same size with the same risk as that involved in the

property in question. . . . The actions of typical buyers and sellers are reflected in the comparison approach.

In essence, the sales comparison approach examines like prop-erties and adjusts value based on similarities and differences. This method is used most often in valuing single-family houses. Let's say, for example, you decide to sell your house. To help you deter-mine a listing price, your sales agent will pull up all of the current listings in your neighborhood, as well as recent sales, and calcu-late a range of prices based on the average sales price per square foot. Then the agent will consider factors such as the overall con-dition and the various amenities of your house. Does it have a fireplace or a swimming pool? Is it a two-car or a three-car garage? And so goes the process, adding and subtracting until a final value is determined. The use of sales comps, as they are called, is the most important factor in the overall analysis of determining the value of single-family properties. It is very much like shopping for a new car. You consider all the alternatives that each manufacturer has to offer, compare each and every feature, and match them to your specific needs. As an investor in value play opportunities, you should rely heavily on the sales comps in your particular market. It is the basis that every buyer looking at your houses will use to make purchase decisions.

In summary, each of the traditional valuation methods serves a unique function by estimating value using one of three different approaches. In some cases, all three approaches may be used, apply-ing varying weights to each. Butler Burgher affirms, "The appraisal process is concluded by a reconciliation of the approaches. This aspect of the process gives consideration to the type and reliability of market data used, the applicability of each approach to the type of property appraised and the type of value sought."

This is the mark of a really admirable man: steadfast-ness in the face of trouble.
                                                        —Ludwig van Beethoven

---

Chapter 6

Financial Analysis

$\mathbb{N}$ow that you have a good understanding of the three primary valuation approaches, let's look at some examples of how to apply them. In particular, we examine more closely how to use the comparable sales approach in estimating the potential resale value of various properties. Then we look at an example in which a multifamily property is converted into individual single-family units. Finally, we examine the conversion of a single-family house to income-producing commercial use and evaluate its effect on the property's value.

THE TEXAS TWO-STEP

More than 20 years ago I bought my very first investment property. I was living in Texas at the time. Actually, I bought two houses at the same time from an older gentleman who had owned the houses for years and had maintained them as rental units. The houses were located in the same neighborhood and were right around the corner from each other. They were about 40 years old and in need of minor repairs such as paint and cleanup. All of the real estate books I had read at the time advocated the traditional buy-and-hold approach, so my intentions were to do exactly that—buy the two houses and hold them, much the same as the gentleman whom

I was buying them from had done. I decided I would spend a little bit of money fixing them up and then rent them out.

The seller owned the two houses free and clear, which means that there were no underlying obligations such as mortgages on them. Since he was retiring, he did not want to sell them for all cash, but instead preferred to receive regular monthly payments. He was more than glad to carry the financing, which worked out well for me. That meant I wouldn't have to bother with getting a mortgage from a more traditional lending source, such as a bank. We agreed on a sales price of $20,000 apiece for the two houses. The deal was structured as shown in Exhibit 6.1.

A few weeks later, we closed on both houses simultaneously, and before I knew it, I was in the real estate business! Since I was young and full of energy at the time, I decided to take on the painting and cleanup myself. I spent the next month painting the exteriors of both houses, cutting down the weeds, mowing the grass, and giving the interiors a thorough cleaning. It didn't take long after that to locate tenants and rent out the houses. Since these were my first two rental houses, I didn't have any property management

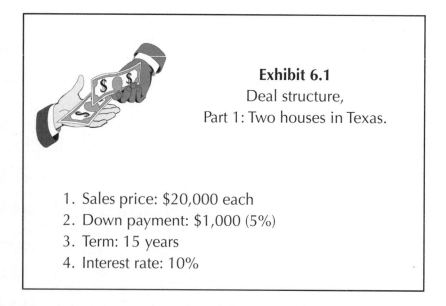

Exhibit 6.1
Deal structure,
Part 1: Two houses in Texas.

1. Sales price: $20,000 each
2. Down payment: $1,000 (5%)
3. Term: 15 years
4. Interest rate: 10%

experience. The only training I had came from a couple of books I had read.

After a few months of being in the rental business, I was beginning to have second thoughts about my new career in real estate. Actually, the tenants weren't that bad. It just seemed to me that this so-called buy-and-hold approach was going to be a long and painstaking process. At the rate I was going, it would be a long time before I could even begin to think about retirement. After about a year, I began to consider the idea of selling the houses to the tenants who lived there and thought about how I could structure the sale in a manner that would be agreeable to them. I decided to carry the note myself, or provide owner financing, as it is sometimes referred to. I agreed to let the tenants apply a portion of the rent they had been paying. Take a look at Exhibit 6.2 to see how the deal was structured.

Now take a minute to study Table 6.1. The worksheet you see is a proprietary model I developed that I use to quickly and easily analyze potential value play investment opportunities. I call it The Value Play Rehab Analyzer. Once I have gathered the necessary

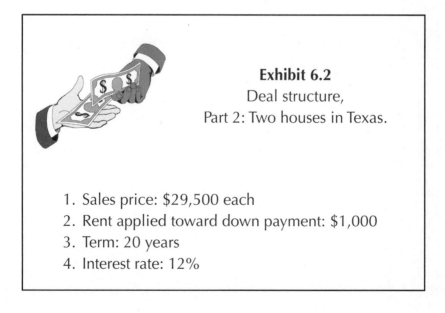

Exhibit 6.2
Deal structure,
Part 2: Two houses in Texas.

1. Sales price: $29,500 each
2. Rent applied toward down payment: $1,000
3. Term: 20 years
4. Interest rate: 12%

Table 6.1 Property Analysis Worksheet: The Value Play Rehab Analyzer

Purchase Assumptions

Project Name:	Two Houses in Texas
Address:	123 South State St.
City, State, Zip:	Baytown, TX 77520
Contact:	Mr. Retired Gentleman
Telephone:	(800) 555-1234

Land	2,500
Building/House	17,500
Closing Costs	500
Other Related Costs	0
Total Purchase Price	20,500

Financing Assumptions—Primary

Primary Mortgage or Loan:

Total Purchase	100.00%	20,500
Down Payment	7.32%	1,500
Balance to Finc	92.68%	19,000

	Annual	Monthly
Interest Rate	10.000%	0.833%
Amort Period	15	180
Payment	2,450	204
Interest Only	1,900	158

Financing Assumptions—Secondary

Secondary Financing/Line of Credit:

Total Imprvmnts	100.00%	1,085
Down Payment	100.00%	1,085
Balance to Finc	0.00%	0

	Annual	Monthly
Interest Rate	8.000%	0.667%
Amort Period	15	180
Payment	0	0
Interest Only	0	0

Estimate for Improvements

Appliances		Flooring		Lighting	0
Dishwasher	0	Carpet	0	Masonry	0
Disposal	0	Ceramic Tile	0	Other	0
Microwave	0	Hardwood	0	Other	0
Range	0	Vinyl	0	Other	0
Refrigerator	0	Subtotal	**0**	Painting: Exterior	450
Subtotal	**0**	Foundation	0	Painting: Interior	0
Architectural Drawings	0	Framing	0	Permits	0
Cabinets	0	Garage	0	Subtotal	**450**
Caulking	25	Gas & Electric Hookup	25	Plumbing	0
Subtotal	**25**	Glass: Mirrors, showers		Commodes	0
Cement Work		Gutters	0	Drain Lines	0
Basement Floor	0	Subtotal	**25**	Faucets	0
Driveway	0	HVAC		Fixtures	0
Garage Floor	0	Air Conditioner	0	Hot Water Heater	0
Porches	0	Duct Work	0	Showers	0
Sidewalks	0	Filters	0	Tubs	0
Subtotal	**0**	Furnace	0	Water Lines	10
		Subtotal	**0**	Subtotal	**10**

Estimate for Improvements

Cleaning	225	Insulation	0	Roofing	0
Counter Tops	0	Insurance Premiums	250	Siding	0
Decorating	0	Subtotal	250	Site Planning & Engineering	0
Doors	0			Steel	0
Drywall	75			Trim	0
Electrical	0	Landscaping		Utility: Gas & Electric	0
Engineering	0	Irrigation System	0	Utility: Water & Sewer	0
Equipment Rental	0	Lot Clearing	0	Warranty	0
Excavation Work	0	Mowing Services	35	Windows	0
Fences	0	Sod	0	Subtotal	0
Fireplace	0	Trees, Plants, & Shrubs	15		
Subtotal	300	Subtotal	50	Total Cost of Improvements	1,085

Comp #1		Comp #2		Comp #3	
Address:		Address:		Address:	
Sales Price	0.00	Sales Price	0.00	Sales Price	0.00
Adjustments to Price	0.00	Adjustments to Price	0.00	Adjustments to Price	0.00
Adjusted Price	0.00	Adjusted Price	0.00	Adjusted Price	0.00
Square Feet	1.00	Square Footage	1.00	Square Feet	1.00
Price Per Square Foot	0.00	Price Per Square Foot	0.00	Price Per Square Foot	0.00

Comp Averages		Subject Property 123 South State St.	
Sales Price	0.00	Square Feet	750.00
Adjustments to Price	0.00	Price/Sq Ft	27.33
Adjusted Price	0.00	Imprvmnts/Sq Ft	1.45
Square Feet	1.00	Total Price/Sq Ft	28.78
Price Per Square Foot	0.00		

		Adjustment to Comps	4.25	
Description	Best Case	Most Likely	Worst Case
Est Sales Price	32,688	29,500	26,313
Purchase Price	20,500	20,500	20,500
Improvements	1,085	1,085	1,085
Interest Charges	0	0	0
Taxes	0	0	0
Closing Costs	350	350	350
Total Costs	21,935	21,935	21,935
Profit Margin	10,753	7,565	4,378
Return On Inv	415.96%	292.65%	169.34%

Turn Comps Off/On	OFF
Est Price/Sq Ft If Turned OFF	39.33
Estimated Time To Complete Project	0.00

data, I can input the information into the model and, in less than five minutes, know within a reasonable degree of accuracy whether a deal makes sense based on my investment criteria. All I have to do is key in the information and the model automatically makes all of the calculations.

Under the Purchase Assumptions section in Table 6.1, the basic property information is listed, including a project name, address, and pricing information. The value of the land does not really matter as long as the price of the land plus the price of the house is equal to the total purchase price. There are two sections for Financing Assumptions—one for primary financing and another one for secondary financing. The primary financing section is used for the main source of lending, which can be a mortgage company, a bank, or a private individual, as this example illustrates. The secondary financing section is used for any additional loans you may secure. For lower-cost improvements, such as the one in this example, you may use all cash. On the other hand, if the cost of the improvements is greater than the amount of capital you want to use, then this is the section to use. Rates and terms are typically different for a line of credit, such as a home equity line or a credit card, than they are for a regular mortgage, so having two sections for financing allows you to more accurately determine your carrying costs.

Under the Estimate for Improvements section, there is quite a bit of detail that allows you to estimate the costs for virtually everything in a house. Estimating these costs accurately is, of course, vitally important for the proper analysis of an investment rehab opportunity. The more experience you have, the easier estimating costs will become. At first, you may need to procure bids or estimates from contractors to help you determine how much the required improvements will cost. As you gain experience, however, you'll be able to estimate many of the costs on your own. The total cost of improvements in this example is only $1,085.

The next section of the model allows you to enter information for comparable home sales. This information is needed to help you make accurate projections of the estimated resale value of your investment property. Any sales agent can provide you with comparable sales data for your area. In addition, a provision in this section allows you to make adjustments to the sales price of the comps, which permits you to compare apples to apples. For example, if the home you are buying has a two-car garage and the comparable home sale has a three-car garage, you will need to revise the price downward in the Adjustments to Price section. This is exactly how real estate agents and appraisers derive the market value of a house. They start with an average price per square foot for several similar houses and make compensating adjustments to estimate value.

The Comp Averages section simply takes an average of the three comps' sales prices to come up with an average sales price. This number is then divided by the average price per square foot. The result is a weighted average price per square foot. This section also has a provision that allows you to turn the comps section off or on. As you become familiar with a specific market or neighborhood, you are likely to already know what the average sales price per square foot is, so you really don't need to key in sales comp data. Instead, you can turn off the comps section and plug in your own estimate. In this example, I had only one comparable sale and that was the house I lived in. I paid $40,000 for a 1,000-square-foot house located in the same neighborhood just a few blocks away. I reasoned that since I paid $40 per square foot for my house and had just had a recent appraisal on it, then I should be able to get close to $40 per square foot for the houses I was selling. I liked the number $29,500 because it was less than $30,000 and sounded more affordable. Therefore, in the example in Table 6.1, the comparable sales section is turned off.

The average sales price per square foot is then fed into the Subject Property section. All of the information keyed into the rest of the model is summarized in this section. You must know the square footage of the house you are buying so that you can make an accurate comparison. The purchase price per square foot is automatically calculated, as is the total cost of the improvements per square foot. The two numbers are then added together to give you the total cost of the project. In this example, the total cost of improvements of $1,085 was added to the total purchase price of

$20,500. The resulting sum was then divided by 750 square feet to give me a total price per square foot of $28.78. Below that is a provision that allows you to estimate the total time (in months) for completion and resale. In other words, it calculates the carrying costs for interest, a factor that many less experienced investors do not consider. In the example here, the number of months is set to zero since the house was occupied as a rental.

The Adjustment to Comps cell is used to create the estimated sales price for three different sales scenarios: best case, most likely, and worst case. In this example, $4.25 per square foot is used. For the best-case sales price, the model adds $4.25 to the price per square foot cell in the Comp Averages section, then multiplies the sum of the two by the square feet of the subject property. Here's how it works:

Best-case sales price

= (average price per square foot + adjustment to comps)

× subject property square feet

= ($39.333 + $4.250) × 750 = $32,688

The most likely sales price calculation in the model neither adds nor subtracts the value of $4.25 to the price per square foot cell in the Comp Averages section. It is simply the product of the average price per square foot and the square feet. Take a moment to examine the following equation:

Most likely sales price

= average price per square foot × subject property square feet

= $39.333 × 750 = $29,500

For the worst-case sales price, the model subtracts $4.25 from the price per square foot in the Comp Averages section, then multiplies the difference between the the two by the square feet of the subject property. Take a minute to review the following equation:

Worst-case sales price

$$= \text{(average price per square foot} - \text{adjustment to comps)}$$

$$\times \text{subject property square feet}$$

$$= (\$39.333 - \$4.250) \times 750 = \$26{,}313$$

The purpose of creating three different scenarios in the model is to provide us with a range for the estimated sales price. This allows you to evaluate the very minimum you might expect on the low end of the price range, and the very most you might expect on the high end of the price range. Take a moment to refer back to Table 6.1. The purchase price, improvements, interest charges, taxes, and closing costs remain constant across all three scenarios since these values are not affected by the adjustment to comps variable of $4.25. The *profit margin* is the dollar amount that you can expect from your investment after all costs have been accounted for. The *return on investment* (ROI) is calculated as the ratio of the profit margin divided by the total cash you have invested in the property. It is calculated as follows for the most likely scenario:

Return on investment

$$= \frac{\text{profit margin}}{\text{primary down payment} + \text{secondary down payment}}$$

$$= \frac{\$7{,}565}{(\$1{,}500 + \$1{,}085)} = 292.65\%$$

My very first investment in the two houses in Texas proved to be a classic example of just how effective the value play strategy can work. I was able to find two houses priced below market that needed minimal repairs from a seller who was willing to carry the note and who also only required $1,000 down on each house. With a little bit of sweat equity on my part, I was able to substantially improve the two houses, rent them out, and later sell them for a respectable profit of $7,565 each. As shown in the preceding calculation, this represented a return of 292.65 percent on my invested capital. Not bad for a rookie.

Since I had not yet developed the Value Play Rehab Analyzer, the output depicted in Table 6.1 was not available to me at that time. Although I had done my homework with respect to market prices and believed that I was purchasing the two houses at a good price, I did not have the foresight to look ahead and determine exactly how much profit could be unlocked from this investment. Selling the houses for a profit early in the game really came as an afterthought. I'm sure you'll agree with me that there is great value in having a dynamic model such as the one illustrated in Table 6.1. By keying in the basic assumptions, you can very easily change a few variables to quickly identify any upside potential. Additional information about the the model used in this example and the ones following may be found in Appendix C.

MULTIPLY YOUR EFFORTS BY 22

Now let's look at another example. Those of you who have read *The Complete Guide to Buying and Selling Apartment Buildings* may recognize this as one of the examples I used in that book. The example is one of a multifamily property I acquired that falls into both the income-producing category and the rehab, or flipping, category. For those readers who have been involved in a condominium conversion, you will understand why. With a condo conversion, you are taking an income property such as an apartment building and converting it to non-income-producing units to be sold on an individual basis. You are removing the income aspect from the property and converting it to a different use; therefore, the valuation method changes from the income capitalization approach to the market comparables approach. This example illustrates how the value play concept can be applied on a larger scale.

Several years ago, I came across a 22-unit multifamily property that at first glance appeared to be very reasonably priced. The seller was asking $350,000. The 22 units consisted of 11 duplex buildings that were lined up neatly in a row side by side. Also included in the sale was an empty lot that was located adjacent to the units. The apartments enjoyed an occupancy of greater than 95 percent with very little turnover. A drive by the property revealed that the buildings had not seen any new paint since their construction approximately 17 years earlier. The lawn was in dire need of attention. Shrubs and hedges lined each building, but had not been trimmed for years. Trees planted in between each driveway offered nice shade for the tenants, but they, too, were overgrown. Each unit had its own private cedar-fenced yard, but, like the worn paint, the fences appeared to be poor condition. So far, this was shaping up to be the kind of deal I liked. Paint, landscaping, and fencing are all fairly inexpensive improvements and could be made quickly.

While the $350,000 asking price sounded very reasonable, I needed something to compare it to that would provide me with an idea of the potential value that could be created after the property was cleaned up. As I drove around the neighborhood, I came across an entire street just a few blocks away that was lined with duplexes very similar to the ones I was looking at. One of them had a For Sale sign out front, so I jotted down the number and returned to my office to inquire about the property. I visited with the seller at length, and it turned out that he represented the owner who had at one time owned all 36 duplex buildings on the street, a total of 72 units. The owner had initially maintained them as rentals, but over the past three years began selling them off to individuals who lived in them or to other investors who rented them out. Out of his original inventory of 72 units, he had sold 68 and now had only four left. His asking price was $39,000 per unit or $77,000 for two units. This information was critical in that it told me two important things. First, the owner had sold 68 units over a three-year period. This meant there was a market for these properties. Second, the price of $77,000 per building had been established and could be used as a valuable comp for appraisal purposes. Since both properties had two bedrooms and two baths and were comparable in size, I knew immediately what the potential upside was. The 22 units I was looking at suddenly began to look very attractive, as the seller was asking only $31,818 per building.

The seller of the 22-unit building I was interested in was a partner in a surveying and engineering company that kept him quite busy. He was not in the apartment business, nor did he care to be. He ended up taking over the duplexes quite by chance. The seller had helped design the project years earlier for an out-of-state investor who eventually came back to him for help in managing the property. As it turned out, the seller ended up taking over the units altogether.

An elderly couple who occupied one of the units served as full-time caretakers, collecting the rents and performing some light maintenance, for which the seller paid them a salary. His objective was to completely minimize his involvement in dealing with tenants, upkeep, and pretty much anything to do with the property. In short, the seller was a bona fide "don't wanter." Fortunately for me, he was not aware of the underlying value that could be unlocked from his property, and even if he were, I don't think he would have been inclined to undergo the process required to create the value. I sincerely believe he was interested only in unloading what had become a source of stress for him.

After brief negotiations with the seller through my real estate broker, I put the duplexes under contract for an agreed-upon price of $333,000. This included all 22 units as well as the vacant tract of land adjacent to them. One unique attribute of this transaction was that all 11 duplex buildings were separately platted and surveyed. This meant that as long as the right type of financing was in place going into the deal, the buildings could all be sold separately or parceled out in any number of ways. For example, an individual could purchase one unit (half of a duplex), two units (all of a duplex), or any combination of units he or she wanted. Proper financing for this type of purchase was a key factor. Most lenders financing multifamily apartments will place a single loan on the entire property and use all of it as collateral. When it comes time to sell, it is either all or none. In other words, you cannot sell off individual units or buildings because the entire purchase is being used to secure the loan or mortgage. After numerous phone calls, I finally found a local bank that was willing to work with me and structure the purchase in a manner that would facilitate my objectives. The loan was set up so that each time I sold a unit, building, or group of buildings, a portion of the loan was paid off and the respective collateral was released to the new lender. As previously mentioned, this transaction was very similar to a condominium conversion, with similar financing being required. The sale was structured as shown in Exhibit 6.3.

As soon as I had the duplexes under contract, I performed the usual due diligence. This included an examination of the seller's record of income collected and expenses paid (e.g., taxes, utilities, and repairs). The next step was a thorough physical inspec-

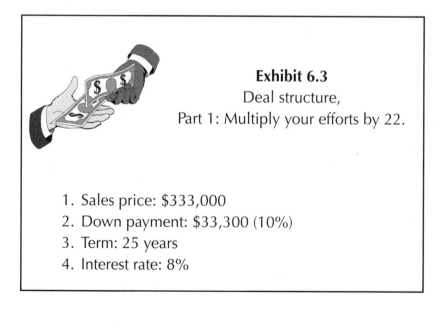

Exhibit 6.3
Deal structure,
Part 1: Multiply your efforts by 22.

1. Sales price: $333,000
2. Down payment: $33,300 (10%)
3. Term: 25 years
4. Interest rate: 8%

tion of each unit inside and out. After carefully examining the property, I was able to assess more precisely the amount of repairs needed to bring the duplexes up to a level I thought was suitable. As was true for the exterior, the needed interior repairs were largely cosmetic. There was the usual—worn carpets, leaky faucets, marred paint—but nothing of major importance.

After I was satisfied with the due diligence, the next step was to order the required third-party reports. This particular lender required a survey, an appraisal, an inspection, and a Phase I environmental report. All reports came in satisfactory. An added bonus was the appraised value, which was determined to be $520,000 with the property in its existing condition. I was, of course, pleased with the report because it served to validate my beliefs about the upside potential that existed in this deal.

After all reports were sent to the lender, a final review of the loan package was completed and subsequently approved. The seller and I closed a few days later. It was truly a win-win situation for all parties involved. The seller was relieved of his headache; I had just purchased a superb value play opportunity; and the banker had made a sound loan. Now the real fun was about to begin. It was time to get to work and unlock the hidden value in this little gem!

I have described at length the entry strategy implemented to acquire the 22 units. Now let's take a look at the postentry process. During the period I had the duplexes under contract, I procured several estimates from contractors for all of the work I wanted performed. Before the deal closed, I had most all of the contractors lined up to begin working the week after the closing. The tenants were notified that the property was under new management and that they would begin seeing some much needed improvements. The flurry of activity actually created some excitement among them, and they were genuinely enthusiastic that someone was finally taking an interest in their community.

The property was a real eyesore when I bought it. My intent was to clean it up and make it as aesthetically appealing as I could for the least amount of money possible. As an investor, my goal was to maximize the use of each and every dollar spent on the project. Over the next 60 to 90 days, the contractors were busy cleaning up the property. My very first priority was to get a professional landscaping crew started. You'd be amazed at what a difference it can make to simply mow down the weeds. They didn't stop there though. They trimmed all of the hedges, edged along the sidewalks, and cleaned up the grounds. I also had the landscaping crew bring in several truckloads of fresh mulch to place around the bushes and hedges. By signing an annual contract with these landscapers, they assumed responsibility for all mowing, hedging, and edging on a weekly basis and at a very reasonable rate. The large, beautiful trees planted in between each of the driveways were so overgrown that they, too, had become an eyesore. A tree-trimming service promptly alleviated that problem. Within a single day, workers had all of the trees trimmed and most of the branches hauled away.

With the landscapers and tree trimmers were busy with their work, I also engaged the services of a painting crew. The painters did an excellent job of painting the exteriors of all 11 buildings, using a combination of four different color schemes to give each building its own unique look while still maintaining a standard of uniformity throughout the community. The painters had the most work to do, and consequently their job took the longest. As previously mentioned, all 11 buildings were side by side. Each one had a fence running down the middle to separate the units, which gave each tenant a small private yard with a gate that could be locked for privacy. Most of the fences were run-down and the gates were barely functional. I had another crew replace all of the worn-out fencing with brand-new cedar fencing. Each unit also got a new entry gate for its backyard. Meanwhile, I hired a sign maker to build signs for the two entryways into the community. There were no signs when I acquired the duplexes, so there was no way for prospective tenants or buyers to call for information. The sign maker built two professional signs out of two-inch-thick redwood and installed one at each entryway. In this manner, the name of the community and the telephone number were prominently displayed.

Since the community was family oriented, I thought a nice amenity to offer the tenants would be a playground where they could bring their children. As it was, there was not any playground equipment close by. I had determined the vacant lot included in the purchase, which was immediately adjacent to the buildings, would be the perfect place for such a playground. I started off by having a concrete crew come in and pour a large 20-by 30-foot slab of concrete, complete with goalposts. This gave the tenants a new basketball court. I also had a company that made professional playground equipment install a swing set, monkey bars, and two animal rides that were mounted on springs and anchored in concrete. For the parents, new vinyl-coated park benches were installed. When all of the work had been completed, the 22 units looked like new and the tenants lived in a complex they could truly take pride in.

I knew before I ever bought the duplexes that my exit strategy would be to either sell or refinance the property within 12 months of purchase. The market research I did before I purchased the duplexes proved to be right on target. Since I had just spent a considerable amount of time and money improving the overall condition of the property, I now had a very attractive community to offer to prospective families.

To unlock the newly created value in the duplexes, I considered several approaches. The first was to sell the units either individually or as a package deal to an investor. My original intent was to sell the units individually for $77,000 per building or $38,500 per unit—similar to the method used by the seller of the other 72 units. With this in mind, I decided to set up one unit as an office that would also double as a model. The initial response from my existing tenants as well as others was quite favorable. Within the first 90 days, I had commitments for 17 of the units. However, I was not prepared for the poor credit quality that most of them had. I was working through a mortgage company that could provide financing for A-, B-, or C-quality paper, but the majority of those who expressed an interest couldn't even come up with the necessary down payment, which was minimal. I could have put together some creative carryback financing of my own, but I really was not interested in doing so at the time. Of the original 17 interested parties, only one made it all the way to closing.

Shortly afterward, I decided to advertise the units in the classified section of the newspaper. I offered them as a package deal to investors. The ad generated quite a bit of interest. I had the remaining 21 units under contract with one investor who assured me he could close the deal in 30 days. As it turned out, he couldn't, and the deal fell out of contract. I then received a call from two investors who were partners. They told me they were interested in all remaining 21 units and wanted to meet me at the property. I agreed to meet with them, but really didn't take them too seriously, as I had already had a number of prospective buyers come by and kick the tires. I initially met with one of the two partners and later met with the second one. As it turned out, the two investors were eager to put a deal together.

I knew that each building would easily appraise for a minimum of $77,000 since I had an entire neighborhood of comps right down the street. Inasmuch as the investors agreed to buy all remaining 21 units in a package deal, I agreed to what was an attractive discount for them, but also left plenty of profit for me. Here's how the deal played out. I agreed to sell each building at a net discounted price of $66,364. Since the buyers were receiving a discount of more than $10,000 per building, they agreed to pay all closing costs. Over the next six to eight months, the buyers followed through and purchased all remaining 21 units from me. It took that long because they used several lenders for their financing. They could have gotten a commercial loan to cover all 21 units, but they would have had to put down 15 to 20 percent. Instead, they placed several single-family housing loans on the property, which provided 90 percent financing rather than the 80 percent a commercial lender would have offered. Furthermore, since the properties appraised for well over the contract price, the buyers did not have to come up with the full 10 percent down payment, because the 90 percent financing was based on the appraised value and not the net sales price. The buyers had to use

Table 6.2 Property Analysis Worksheet: The Value Play Rehab Analyzer

Purchase Assumptions		Financing Assumptions—Primary			Financing Assumptions—Secondary		
Project Name:	Multiply Your Efforts By 22	Primary Mortgage or Loan:			Secondary Financing/Line of Credit:		
Address:	123 South State St.	Total Purchase	100.00%	350,000	Total Imprvmnts	100.00%	60,000
City, State, Zip:	Houston, TX 77520	Down Payment	10.00%	35,000	Down Payment	25.00%	15,000
Contact:	Mr. I Don't Want Her	Balance to Finc	90.00%	315,000	Balance to Finc	75.00%	45,000
Telephone:	(800) 555-9876						
			Annual	Monthly		Annual	Monthly
Land	50,000	Interest Rate	8.000%	0.667%	Interest Rate	8.000%	0.667%
Building/House	283,000	Amort Period	25	300	Amort Period	25	300
Closing Costs	10,000	Payment	29,175	2,431	Payment	4,168	347
Other Related Costs	7,000	Interest Only	25,200	2,100	Interest Only	3,600	300
Total Purchase Price	350,000						

Estimate for Improvements

Appliances		Flooring		Lighting	0
Dishwasher	1,000	Carpet	4,200	Masonry	0
Disposal	250	Ceramic Tile	0	Other—Playground Equipment	15,000
Microwave	0	Hardwood	0	Other—Signage	5,000
Range	500	Vinyl	1,450	Other	0
Refrigerator	0	Subtotal	5,650	Painting: Exterior	12,000
Subtotal	1,750			Painting: Interior	0
		Foundation	0	Permits	0
Architectural Drawings	0	Framing	0	Subtotal	32,000
Cabinets	0	Garage	0		
Caulking	0	Gas & Electric Hookup	0	Plumbing	
Subtotal	0	Glass: Mirrors, showers	0	Commodes	0
		Gutters	0	Drain Lines	0
Cement Work		Subtotal	0	Faucets	0
Basement Floor	0			Fixtures	0
Driveway	1,200	HVAC		Hot Water Heater	0
Garage Floor	0	Air Conditioner	1,800	Showers	0
Porches	0	Duct Work	0	Tubs	0
Sidewalks	0	Filters	50	Water Lines	0
Subtotal	1,200	Furnace	700	Subtotal	0
		Subtotal	2,550		

Estimate for Improvements

Cleaning	800	Insulation	0
Counter Tops	0	Insurance Premiums	0
Decorating	0	**Subtotal**	**0**
Doors	450		
Drywall	0	Landscaping	
Electrical	0	Irrigation System	0
Engineering	0	Lot Clearing	350
Equipment Rental	600	Mowing Services	400
Excavation Work	0	Sod	0
Fences	7,000	Trees, Plants, & Shrubs	7,250
Fireplace	0	**Subtotal**	**8,000**
Subtotal	**8,850**		

Roofing		0
Siding		0
Site Planning & Engineering		0
Steel		
Trim		
Utility: Gas & Electric		0
Utility: Water & Sewer		0
Warranty		0
Windows		0
Subtotal		**0**
Total Cost of Improvements		**60,000**

Comp #1
Address:

Sales Price	Per duplex bld	77,000.00
Adjustments to Price		0.00
Adjusted Price		77,000.00
Square Feet		2,000.00
Price Per Square Foot		38.50

Comp #2
Address:

Sales Price	Per duplex bldg	77,500.00
Adjustments to Price		0.00
Adjusted Price		77,500.00
Square Footage		2,000.00
Price Per Square Foot		38.75

Comp #3
Address:

Sales Price	Per duplex bld	78,000.00
Adjustments to Price		0.00
Adjusted Price		78,000.00
Square Feet		2,000.00
Price Per Square Foot		39.00

Comp Averages

Sales Price	77,500.00
Adjustments to Price	0.00
Adjusted Price	77,500.00
Square Feet	2,000.00
Price Per Square Foot	38.75
Turn Comps Off/On	OFF
Est Price/Sq Ft If Turned OFF	33.47

Subject Property
123 South State St.

Square Feet	22,000.00
Price/Sq Ft	15.91
Imprvmnts/Sq Ft	2.73
Total Price/Sq Ft	18.64
Estimated Time To Complete Project	0.00

Description	Adjustment to Comps	5.28	
	Best Case	Most Likely	Worst Case
Est Sales Price	852,500	736,318	620,136
Purchase Price	350,000	350,000	350,000
Improvements	60,000	60,000	60,000
Interest Charges	0	0	0
Taxes	0	0	0
Closing Costs	0	0	0
Total Costs	410,000	410,000	410,000
Profit Margin	442,500	326,318	210,136
Return On Inv	885.00%	652.64%	420.27%

several lenders because the lenders' underwriting guidelines did not permit them to loan money on more than a maximum of four units to any one individual. Although their decision to use this type of financing prolonged the sale, they did follow through. Within a year of my purchase, I had sold all 22 units. Take a look at Exhibit 6.4 to see how the deal was structured.

On the one hand, my willingness to take less than the appraised value meant that I would leave a lot of money on the table. On the other hand, however, it allowed me to offer a very attractive deal to two willing buyers who could purchase the property with very little money down and have built-in equity on the day of closing. Take a moment to study Table 6.2.

After reviewing Table 6.2, you can see that this is another powerful example of the potential of the value play strategy. This strategy can obviously be quite effective. In this case, my out-of-pocket capital would have been about $100,000; however, since the bank financed 75 percent of the cost of improvements, I ended up tying up about $50,000 of my own money. The total increase in value to

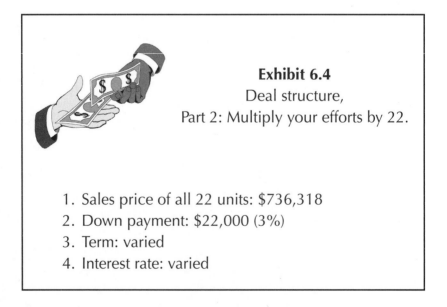

Exhibit 6.4
Deal structure,
Part 2: Multiply your efforts by 22.

1. Sales price of all 22 units: $736,318
2. Down payment: $22,000 (3%)
3. Term: varied
4. Interest rate: varied

the property was almost 80 percent (($736,318 − $410,000)/ $410,000). By using some very basic techniques that are fundamental to the value play strategy, I was able to effectively increase the value of the property by more than twice the original sales price that I had paid. Although I may have left money on the table for the two investors, there was still plenty left in it for me. In about a year's time, I netted over $326,000 from the deal. While it is true that I could have held out for another buyer who may have been willing to pay full price, I place a lot of faith in the old adage that a bird in the hand is worth two in the bush.

FROM RESIDENTIAL TO COMMERCIAL

Now let's look at a conversion process that is exactly the opposite of the previous example. In the case of the 22 duplex units, the property was converted from an income-producing property to that of a single-family residential. Even though two investors ended up buying the majority of the units, it was still valued by using a market comparison approach rather than an income approach. In this example, we will study the conversion of a single-family residence to a commercial income-producing property and examine the differences in the two valuation approaches.

The house in this example is one that I currently have under contract to purchase. It is located in the downtown area of a small but growing community with a population of about 42,000 residents. The street on which it is located is actually a state highway that runs right through the heart of the city. It is considered to be a high-traffic location, with an average daily traffic count of about 22,000 vehicles. When the house was originally built back in 1903, it was probably inconceivable at the time that the street running in front of the house would eventually become a state highway. It is a very charming two-story house with approximately 2,400 square feet of living space. There is a large basement that can be used for storage. The house has been fairly well maintained over the years (although some work is needed), and the inside is full of charm and character reminiscent of a bygone era. It has a beautiful handcrafted wooden stairway leading to the upstairs and many other features characteristic of early-1900s architecture.

For literally the past 100 years, the house has been occupied as a residence. The current owner has lived there since 1980, and even since then, there has been significant growth in the area. The owner had been trying to sell the house for nearly a year with the assistance of a real estate agent, but with no success. With new communities springing up all around, who wants to live on busy state highway? Not many people, that's for sure. You can just about rule out any family with small children. Being that close to a busy road would be too dangerous for little ones. Rule out the seniors, too. They prefer quiet communities with sidewalks and streetlights. Who does that leave? No one, really, except maybe a guy like me looking for cheap office space.

The house is actually in an ideal location for an office building. The high-traffic location is particularly appealing in that it will enable our company, Symphony Homes, to greatly increase its brand identity and name recognition in that market. Approximately 22,000 motorists will pass by our brightly lit sign each and every day, 365 days a year. As they do, they will become more and more familiar with our name. Eventually, many of them will come to us seeking the services we offer. With 2,400 square feet, the building is large enough to meet our current needs. In addition, it is much cheaper than leasing office or retail space in the same area, and certainly much cheaper than purchasing office or retail space.

As previously mentioned, this is why understanding the differences of the three market valuation approaches is so important. If you can grasp the underlying logic and understand the fundamental principles of each method, you can use them to your advantage to create value. In its current state of use as a single-family house, the most appropriate valuation method is to use the comparable sales approach. This is the method that will be used when the appraiser comes out to appraise the property. He will examine like properties, make adjustments as necessary, and derive a value that is most appropriate for this property in its current state of use. When the house is converted to an income-producing office building, its usage will change from residential to commercial. At that time, the value of the building will no longer be based on comparable sales of similar houses. Instead, it will be based on the income generated from the rents, in which case the income capitalization approach will be the most appropriate method of valuing the property.

My objective going into this transaction is, as always, to apply the OPM principle—that is, to use as much of other people's money as possible and as little of my own money as possible. Since the house is literally a century old, it is in need of some repair work. There will also be additional costs involved to convert the property from residential to commercial use. The owner and I agreed on a sales price of $188,000, with a repair and/or improvement allowance of $40,000, making the effective sales price $148,000. Since I will borrow 90 percent of the sales price, my down payment will only be 10 percent, or $18,000. At closing, I will receive an allowance for the necessary repairs and improvements in the amount of $40,000. Now take a look at Exhibit 6.5 to see how the deal was structured.

Structuring the transaction in this manner will allow me to limit the amount of out-of-pocket cash to only 10 percent of the total deal value, including the improvements. This is a creative and effective way to pull cash out of a deal at closing, especially when you have an immediate use for the cash such as for property improvements. To use this financing strategy, you should be aware of two caveats. The first is that the house has to appraise for a high enough value in its existing condition. In this example, the house must appraise for the sales price of $188,000 before any repairs or improvements are made. That means there must be existing comparable sales the appraiser can use to support the value. We are already aware of several comps that will support the sales price. The second caveat is that you must have a lender who is willing to work with you in allowing the credit at closing.

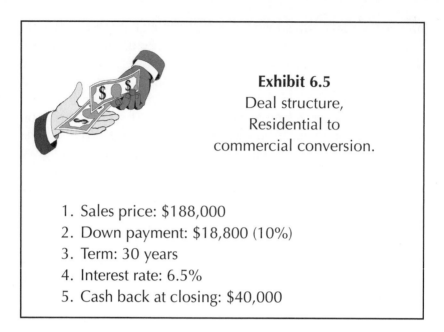

Exhibit 6.5
Deal structure,
Residential to
commercial conversion.

1. Sales price: $188,000
2. Down payment: $18,800 (10%)
3. Term: 30 years
4. Interest rate: 6.5%
5. Cash back at closing: $40,000

While most lenders will allow the buyer to receive some type of credit, they generally limit it to anywhere from 3 to 5 percent of the sales price. I usually have the most success using a mortgage broker when trying to structure a deal like this rather than going directly to a lender. Many small community banks, however, will work with you as long as they understand what you are trying to do. In addition, they may require the funds credited at closing to be placed into an escrow account and paid only after the work has been completed. Now take a moment to examine Table 6.3.

In the Purchase Assumptions box, I used $152,000 ($33,000 + $115,000 + $3,650 + $350) for the purchase price since that is the net effective sales price of the house. The loan terms for the purchase price are reflected in the Financing Assumptions (Primary) box. The total of $40,000 for improvements has been entered into the Estimate for Improvements section and is captured in Financing Assumptions (Secondary). In this case, since the primary and secondary financing will be combined into one note, the same interest rate and term is used. To calculate the total payment, simply add the two together. The information in the Comp Averages section suggests a weighted average price per square foot of $81.92. When multiplied by 2,400 square feet, the resulting value is $196,609, which is well above the required value of $188,000 necessary to make the deal work. After factoring in transactions costs, the profit margin in the most likely scenario reflects a small profit of $712. Remember that the value shown here is *before* any improvements have been made. Now let's take a few minutes to study Table 6.4. Although this model is similar to The Value Play Rehab Analyzer, it is really quite different. This model is The Value Play Income Analyzer and is used to measure the value of an income-producing property such as an apartment building—or our soon-to-be-converted office building.

In Table 6.4, notice that we have the same sales price of $148,000 plus $40,000 in improvements, plus $4,000 in closing costs and other costs for a total of $192,000 just as we did in Table 6.3. Notice also that the information in the Financing Assumptions is exactly the same, except for the fact that it is consolidated into one section rather than two. The Key Ratios section in Table 6.4 captures important data relative to an income-producing property. The most important number to focus on for this example is the capitalization rate. The capitalization rate, or *cap rate* as it is referred to, is the ratio between net operating income and sales price:

$$\textit{Capitalization rate}$$

$$= \frac{\text{net operating income}}{\text{sales price}}$$

or

$$\textit{Sales price}$$

$$= \frac{\text{net operating income}}{\text{cap rate}}$$

Table 6.3 Property Analysis Worksheet: The Value Play Rehab Analyzer

Purchase Assumptions

Project Name:	Residential to Commercial
Address:	123 South State St.
City, State, Zip:	Anywhere, TX 77520
Contact:	Mr. Please Buy My House
Telephone:	(800) 555-1234

Land	33,000
Building/House	115,000
Closing Costs	3,650
Other Related Costs	350
Total Purchase Price	152,000

Financing Assumptions—Primary

Primary Mortgage or Loan:

Total Purchase	100.00%	152,000
Down Payment	10.00%	15,200
Balance to Finc	90.00%	136,800

	Annual	Monthly
Interest Rate	6.500%	0.542%
Amort Period	30	360
Payment	10,376	865
Interest Only	8,892	741

Financing Assumptions—Secondary

Secondary Financing/Line of Credit:

Total Imprvmnts	100.00%	40,000
Down Payment	10.00%	4,000
Balance to Finc	90.00%	36,000

	Annual	Monthly
Interest Rate	6.500%	0.542%
Amort Period	30	360
Payment	2,731	228
Interest Only	2,340	195

Estimate for Improvements

Appliances				
Dishwasher	0			
Disposal	0			
Microwave	0			
Range	0			
Refrigerator	0			
Subtotal		**0**		

Architectural Drawings	0		
Cabinets	0		
Caulking	450		
Subtotal		**450**	

Cement Work			
Basement Floor	0		
Driveway	0		
Garage Floor	0		
Porches	0		
Sidewalks	1,200		
Subtotal		**1,200**	

Flooring			
Carpet	2,000		
Ceramic Tile	0		
Hardwood	0		
Vinyl	1,500		
Subtotal		**3,500**	

Foundation	0		
Framing	0		
Garage	500		
Gas & Electric Hookup	0		
Glass: Mirrors, showers	0		
Gutters	0		
Subtotal		**500**	

HVAC			
Air Conditioner	1,800		
Duct Work	0		
Filters	25		
Furnace	225		
Subtotal		**2,050**	

Lighting	750		
Masonry	0		
Parking Lot & Drive	8,400		
Other	0		
Other	0		
Painting: Exterior	1,200		
Painting: Interior	2,100		
Permits	250		
Subtotal		**12,700**	

Plumbing			
Commodes	0		
Drain Lines	0		
Faucets	250		
Fixtures	250		
Hot Water Heater	0		
Showers	0		
Tubs	0		
Water Lines	0		
Subtotal		**500**	

Estimate for Improvements

Cleaning	1,000	Insulation	0	Roofing	7,800
Counter Tops	0	Insurance Premiums	525	Siding	0
Decorating	1,500	Subtotal	525	Site Planning & Engineering	2,200
Doors	500			Steel	0
Drywall	250	Landscaping		Trim	0
Electrical	500	Irrigation System	0	Utility: Gas & Electric	250
Engineering	0	Lot Clearing	0	Utility: Water & Sewer	125
Equipment Rental	0	Mowing Services	50	Warranty	0
Excavation Work	0	Sod	0	Windows	500
Fences	2,500	Trees, Plants, & Shrubs	1,400	Subtotal	10,875
Fireplace	0	Subtotal	1,450		
Subtotal	6,250			Total Cost of Improvements	40,000

Comp #1		Comp #2		Comp #3	
Address:		Address:		Address:	
Sales Price	179,900.00	Sales Price	186,500.00	Sales Price	189,450.00
Adjustments to Price	1,200.00	Adjustments to Price	1,800.00	Adjustments to Price	(2,200.00)
Adjusted Price	181,100.00	Adjusted Price	188,300.00	Adjusted Price	187,250.00
Square Feet	2,200.00	Square Footage	2,320.00	Square Feet	2,275.00
Price Per Square Foot	82.32	Price Per Square Foot	81.16	Price Per Square Foot	82.31

Comp Averages		Subject Property 123 South State St.	
Sales Price	185,283.33	Square Feet	2,400.00
Adjustments to Price	266.67	Price/Sq Ft	63.33
Adjusted Price	185,550.00	Imprvmnts/Sq Ft	16.67
Square Feet	2,265.00	Total Price/Sq Ft	80.00
Price Per Square Foot	81.92		

Description	Adjustment to Comps 5.00		
	Best Case	Most Likely	Worst Case
Est Sales Price	208,609	196,609	184,609
Purchase Price	152,000	152,000	152,000
Improvements	40,000	40,000	40,000
Interest Charges	1,872	1,872	1,872
Taxes	450	450	450
Closing Costs	1,575	1,575	1,575
Total Costs	195,897	195,897	195,897
Profit Margin	12,712	712	(11,288)
Return On Inv	66.21%	3.71%	-58.79%

Turn Comps Off/On	ON	
Est Price/Sq Ft If Turned OFF	80.00	
Estimated Time To Complete Project	2.00	

Table 6.4 Property Analysis Worksheet: The Value Play Income Analyzer

Cost and Revenue Assumptions

Land	33,000
Building	115,000
Improvements	40,000
Closing Costs	4,000
Total	192,000
Number of Units	1
Average Monthly Rent	2,400
Gross Monthly Revenues	2,400

Financing Assumptions

Total Purchase	192,000	100.00%
Owner's Equity	19,200	10.00%
Balance to Finc	172,800	90.00%

	Annual	Monthly
Interest Rate	6.500%	0.542%
Amort Period	30	360
Payment	13,107	1,092

Key Ratios

Total Square Feet	2,400.00
Avg Sq Ft/Unit	2,400.00
Avg Rent/Sq Ft	1.00
Avg Cost/Sq Ft	80.00
Avg Unit Cost	192,000.00
Capitalization Rate	14.25%
Gross Rent Multiplier	6.67
Expense/Unit	0.00
Expense/Foot	0.00

Projections

	Year 1	Year 2	Year 3	Year 4	Year 5
Rental Increase Projections	0.00%	4.00%	4.00%	4.00%	4.00%
Average Monthly Rent	2,400	2,496	2,596	2,700	2,808
Operating Expense Projections	0.00%	0.00%	0.00%	0.00%	0.00%

Operating Revenues

		Actual Monthly	Year 1	Year 2	Projected Year 3	Year 4	Year 5
Gross Scheduled Income		2,400	28,800	29,952	31,150	32,396	33,692
Vacancy Rate	5.0%	120	1,440	1,498	1,558	1,620	1,685
Net Rental Income		2,280	27,360	28,454	29,593	30,776	32,007
Other Income		0	0	0	0	0	0
Gross Income	100.0%	2,280	27,360	28,454	29,593	30,776	32,007

Operating Expenses

		Actual Monthly	Year 1	Year 2	Year 3	Year 4	Year 5
Repairs and Maintenance	0.0%	0	0	0	0	0	0
Property Management Fees	0.0%	0	0	0	0	0	0
Taxes	0.0%	0	0	0	0	0	0
Insurance	0.0%	0	0	0	0	0	0
Salaries and Wages	0.0%	0	0	0	0	0	0
Utilities	0.0%	0	0	0	0	0	0
Trash Removal	0.0%	0	0	0	0	0	0
Professional Fees	0.0%	0	0	0	0	0	0
Advertising	0.0%	0	0	0	0	0	0
Other	0.0%	0	0	0	0	0	0
Total Op. Exp.	0.0%	0	0	0	0	0	0

Net Operating Income	100.0%	2,280	27,360	28,454	29,593	30,776	32,007
Interest on Loan	41.1%	936	11,175	11,046	10,908	10,761	10,603
Dep. Exp.—Building		348	4,182	4,182	4,182	4,182	4,182
Dep. Exp.—Equip.		0	0	0	0	0	0
Net Income Before Taxes		996	12,003	13,227	14,503	15,834	17,222
Income Tax Rate	0.0%	0	0	0	0	0	0
Net Income After Taxes		996	12,003	13,227	14,503	15,834	17,222
Cash Flow From Operations							
Net Income After Taxes		996	12,003	13,227	14,503	15,834	17,222
Dep. Exp.		348	4,182	4,182	4,182	4,182	4,182
Total CF From Ops.		1,344	16,185	17,409	18,685	20,016	21,404
Interest on Loan		936	11,175	11,046	10,908	10,761	10,603
Total Cash Available for Loan Servicing		2,280	27,360	28,454	29,593	30,776	32,007
Debt Service		1,092	13,107	13,107	13,107	13,107	13,107
Remaining After Tax CF From Ops		1,188	14,253	15,348	16,486	17,670	18,901
Plus Principal Reduction		161	1,931	2,061	2,199	2,346	2,503
Total Return		1,349	16,185	17,409	18,685	20,016	21,404
CF/Debt Servicing Ratio		208.75%	208.75%	217.10%	225.78%	234.82%	244.21%
Net Income ROI			62.52%	68.89%	75.54%	82.47%	89.70%
Cash ROI			74.24%	79.94%	85.86%	92.03%	98.44%
Total ROI			84.30%	90.67%	97.32%	104.25%	111.48%
Net CFs From Investment—1 Yr Exit		(19,200)	135,385				
Net CFs From Investment—3 Yr Exit		(19,200)	14,253	15,348	161,877		
Net CFs From Investment—5 Yr Exit		(19,200)	14,253	15,348	16,486	17,670	199,141

	Exit Price	Gain on Sale	Cap Rate
Estimated Exit Price/Gain On Sale—1 Yr	292,000	100,000	9.37%
Estimated Exit Price/Gain On Sale—3 Yr	312,000	120,000	9.48%
Estimated Exit Price/Gain On Sale—5 Yr	342,000	150,000	9.36%

	IRR
Annualized IRR—1 Yr	605.13%
Annualized IRR—3 Yr	146.02%
Annualized IRR—5 Yr	104.29%

As you can see, this ratio is really a very simple calculation used to measure the relationship between the income generated by the property and the price it is being sold for. This ratio measures the same relationship as that of the certificate of deposit we discussed in Chapter 5. The *price* we are willing to pay for the CD is a function of its *yield,* or rather, the *income* the instrument generates. This is precisely consistent with the relationship between the *price* of an income-producing property, the *yield* an investor expects to receive on his or her investment, and the property's ability to generate *income.*

The capitalization rate, or yield on an income-producing property, will vary within a given range, generally 8 to 12 percent depending on a variety of market conditions, including supply and demand for real estate, the current interest rate environment, the type and condition of the property, its location, and tax implications imposed by local, state, and federal authorities. Under the Key Ratios section in Table 6.4, notice the cap rate of 14.25 percent. This number represents the yield of the property as a whole since it is based on the sales price and not the equity. Remember that return on investment (ROI) measures that relationship. A yield of 14.25 percent would be exceptional on a certificate of deposit. It is also considered high on real estate. This indicates the property's sales price is low relative to its ability to generate income. Translated, it means we are buying the property at a bargain price and that there is plenty of upside in the deal.

The average monthly rent is based on a rate of $1 per square foot per month, or $12 per square foot annually, multiplied by the square feet of the house, which gives us $2,400 of rental income per month. In the market in which the building is located, that rate is a conservative number. A vacancy rate of 5 percent is applied for lender purposes. Since the lease will be a net lease, there are no expenses, as they will all be paid by the tenant. Now take a look at the bottom of Table 6.4 at the three different estimated exit prices. Based on the information we know to be true regarding market rates and capitalization rates, we can sell the property at the end of year 1 at an exit price of $292,000 at a very conservative cap rate of 9.37 percent, which will produce a very nice gain on sale of $100,000, excluding transaction costs. The internal rate of return (IRR) is derived by measuring the rate of return over time given a series of cash flows (taken from net CFs from investment, one year exit). In this example, the IRR is an astounding 605 percent in year 1! For those of you who think this kind of return is wishful thinking, may I remind you that these numbers are actually quite conservative and are on the low end of the market based on the rate of $12 per square foot. Now take a moment to study Table 6.5, the Refinance Analyzer.

The Refinance Analyzer provides you with an alternative to selling your income-producing property. Given a certain set of assumptions, it calculates the maximum loan amount that an investor could borrow based on the income produced by the property. In Table 6.5, the maximum loan amount based on an 80 percent loan-to-value (LTV) ratio is $228,540. It also tells us that we have to be able to get an appraisal in the amount of $285,675, which shouldn't be too difficult based on the cap rate of 9.577 percent indicated in the Key Ratios section. Since the new loan would be a commercial loan and not a residential mortgage, I applied a higher interest rate of 7.5 percent and a shorter amortization period of 25 years. Okay, so you can refinance the property. Big deal, right? Let's see just what the effect of our handiwork is:

NEW LOAN AMOUNT:	$228,540
PAY OFF EXISTING LOAN:	$172,800
CASH BACK TO INVESTOR:	$55,740

Refinancing the property based on the income approach has allowed us to justify a much higher value than the one based on the comparable sales approach. In this example, refinancing would put $55,740 cash back in your pocket I'm sure you would agree that you can find something to do with that much money!

Let's look at one more example. We'll make a quick change in

Table 6.5 Refinance Analyzer

Maximum Refinance—Cash Out			Key Ratios	
Max Refinance	80.00%	228,540	Total Square Feet	2,400.000
Owner's Equity @	20.00%	57,135	Avg Sq Ft/Unit	2,400.000
Required Appraisal	100.00%	285,675	Avg Rent/Sq Ft	1.000
			Avg Cost/Sq Ft	119.031
	Annual	Monthly	Avg Unit Cost	285,674,738
Interest Rate	7.500%	0.625%	Capitalization Rate	9.577%
Amortization Period	25	300	Gross Rent Multiplier	9.919
Payment	20,267	1,689	Expense/Unit	0.000
			Expense/Foot	0.000

Operating Revenues		Year 1
Gross Scheduled Income		28,800
Vacancy rate		1,440
Net Rental Income		27,360
Other Income		0
Gross Revenues	100.0%	27,360

Refinance Matrix	
Max Refinance	CF/DS
308,529	100.0%
302,479	102.0%
296,662	104.0%
291,065	106.0%
285,675	108.0%
280,481	110.0%
275,472	112.0%
270,639	114.0%
265,973	116.0%
261,465	118.0%
257,107	120.0%
252,892	122.0%
248,813	124.0%
244,864	126.0%
241,038	128.0%
237,330	130.0%
233,734	132.0%
230,245	134.0%
226,859	136.0%
223,572	138.0%
220,378	140.0%
217,274	142.0%
214,256	144.0%
211,321	146.0%
208,465	148.0%
205,686	150.0%
202,979	152.0%
200,343	154.0%
197,775	156.0%
195,271	158.0%
192,830	160.0%
190,450	162.0%
188,127	164.0%
185,861	166.0%
183,648	168.0%
181,487	170.0%
179,377	172.0%

Operating Expenses		
Repairs and Maintenance	0.0%	0
Property Management Fees	0.0%	0
Taxes	0.0%	0
Insurance	0.0%	0
Salaries and Wages	0.0%	0
Utilities	0.0%	0
Trash Removal	0.0%	0
Professional Fees	0.0%	0
Advertising	0.0%	0
Other	0.0%	0
Total Op. Exp.	0.0%	0

Net Operation Income	100.0%	27,360
Dep. Exp.—Building		4,182
Dep. Exp.—Equip.		0
Net Income Before Taxes		23,178
Income Tax Rate	0.0%	0
Net Income After Taxes		23,178

Cash Flow From Operations		
Net Income After Taxes		23,178
Dep. Exp.		4,182
Total Cash Available for Loan Servicing		27,360
Debt Service		20,267
Remaining After Tax CF From Ops		7,093
Plus Principle Reduction		3,236
Total Return		10,329
CF/Debt Servicing Ratio		135.0%

the Income Analyzer by adjusting the rental income from $12 per square foot to $16 per square foot, which is at the upper end of market rates, to see how that affects the property's value. All other assumptions remain the same. Take a minute to review Table 6.6.

As you can see, by increasing the rents, we are significantly increasing the value of the property. This is similar to increasing the income generated by a certificate of deposit. Since the yield is held constant, the value of the certificate must be increased. With the cap rate in the Income Analyzer held constant at about 9.5 percent, the estimated exit price increases from $292,000 in Table 6.4 to $385,000 in Table 6.6. If the property is sold at the end of year 1, the estimated gain on sale is $193,000, which represents an increase of $93,000 more than the estimated gain on sale in Table 6.4. We now have two different versions, or scenarios, of this property—one at the lower end of the income-per-square-foot range and one at the higher end of the income-per-square-foot range. This provides us with a broad spectrum of values ranging $292,000 to $385,000. These values are a direct function of the income produced by the property, so the higher the rental income that can be justified by local market rates, the more valuable the property. Now let's examine the effect of these changes in our Refinance Analyzer in Table 6.7.

The same assumptions we used in the example in Table 6.5 have been applied to the model in Table 6.7. The maximum loan amount based on an 80 percent LTV ratio is $304,720. The output also tells us that we have to be able to get an appraisal in the amount of $380,900 based on holding the cap rate constant at 9.577 percent as indicated in the Key Ratios box. Here's how it looks:

NEW LOAN AMOUNT:	**$304,720**
PAY OFF EXISTING LOAN:	**$172,800**
CASH BACK TO INVESTOR:	**$131,920**

In this instance, we are able to obtain a new loan in the amount of $304,720, pay off the old loan of $172,800, and pocket the

Table 6.6 Property Analysis Worksheet: The Value Play Income Analyzer

Cost and Revenue Assumptions		Financing Assumptions			Key Ratios	
Land	33,000	Total Purchase	192,000	100.00%	Total Square Feet	2,400.00
Building	115,000	Owner's Equity	19,200	10.00%	Avg Sq Ft/Unit	2,400.00
Improvements	40,000	Balance to Finc	172,800	90.00%	Avg Rent/Sq Ft	1.33
Closing Costs	4,000				Avg Cost/Sq Ft	80.00
Total	192,000				Avg Unit Cost	192,000.00
			Annual	Monthly	Capitalization Rate	19.00%
Number of Units	1	Interest Rate	6.500%	0.542%	Gross Rent Multiplier	5.00
Average Monthly Rent	3,200	Amort Period	30	360	Expense/Unit	0.00
Gross Monthly Revenues	3,200	Payment	13,107	1,092	Expense/Foot	0.00

		Year 1	Year 2	Year 3	Year 4	Year 5
Rental Increase Projections		0.00%	4.00%	4.00%	4.00%	4.00%
Average Monthly Rent		3,200	3,328	3,461	3,600	3,744
Operating Expense Projections		0.00%	0.00%	0.00%	0.00%	0.00%

		Actual			Projected	
Operating Revenues		Monthly	Year 1	Year 2	Year 3	Year 4	Year 5
		Actual Monthly	Year 1	Year 2	Year 3	Year 4	Year 5

Operating Revenues		Actual Monthly	Year 1	Year 2	Year 3	Year 4	Year 5
Gross Scheduled Income		3,200	38,400	39,936	41,533	43,195	44,923
Vacancy Rate	5.0%	160	1,920	1,997	2,077	2,160	2,246
Net Rental Income		3,040	36,480	37,939	39,457	41,035	42,676
Other Income		0	0	0	0	0	0
Gross Income	100.0%	3,040	36,480	37,939	39,457	41,035	42,676

Operating Expenses

Repairs and Maintenance	0.0%	0	0	0	0	0	0
Property Management Fees	0.0%	0	0	0	0	0	0
Taxes	0.0%	0	0	0	0	0	0
Insurance	0.0%	0	0	0	0	0	0
Salaries and Wages	0.0%	0	0	0	0	0	0
Utilities	0.0%	0	0	0	0	0	0
Trash Removal	0.0%	0	0	0	0	0	0
Professional Fees	0.0%	0	0	0	0	0	0
Advertising	0.0%	0	0	0	0	0	0
Other	0.0%	0	0	0	0	0	0
Total Op. Exp.	0.0%	0	0	0	0	0	0

Net Operating Income	100.0%	3,040	36,480	37,939	39,457	41,035	42,676
Interest on Loan	30.8%	936	11,175	11,046	10,908	10,761	10,603
Dep. Exp.—Building		348	4,182	4,182	4,182	4,182	4,182
Dep. Exp.—Equip.		0	0	0	0	0	0
Net Income Before Taxes		1,756	21,123	22,712	24,367	26,093	27,891
Income Tax Rate	0.0%	0	0	0	0	0	0
Net Income After Taxes		1,756	21,123	22,712	24,367	26,093	27,891

Cash Flow From Operations

Net Income After Taxes	1,756	21,123	22,712	24,367	26,093	27,891
Dep. Exp.	348	4,182	4,182	4,182	4,182	4,182
Total CF From Ops.	2,104	25,305	26,893	28,549	30,275	32,073
Interest on Loan	936	11,175	11,046	10,908	10,761	10,603
Total Cash Available for Loan Servicing	3,040	36,480	37,939	39,457	41,035	42,676
Debt Service	1,092	13,107	13,107	13,107	13,107	13,107
Remaining After Tax CF From Ops	1,948	23,373	24,833	26,350	27,928	29,570
Plus Principal Reduction	161	1,931	2,061	2,199	2,346	2,503
Total Return	2,109	25,305	26,893	28,549	30,275	32,073
CF/Debt Servicing Ratio	278.33%	278.33%	289.47%	301.05%	313.09%	325.61%
Net Income ROI		110.02%	118.29%	126.91%	135.90%	145.27%
Cash ROI		121.74%	129.34%	137.24%	145.46%	154.01%
Total ROI		131.80%	140.07%	148.69%	157.68%	167.05%
Net CFs From Investment—1 Yr Exit	(19,200)	237,505				
Net CFs From Investment—3 Yr Exit	(19,200)	23,373	24,833	274,741		
Net CFs From Investment—5 Yr Exit	(19,200)	23,373	24,833	26,350	27,928	317,810

	Exit Price	Gain on Sale	Cap Rate		IRR
Estimated Exit Price/Gain On Sale—1 Yr	385,000	193,000	9.48%	Annualized IRR—1 Yr	1137.00%
Estimated Exit Price/Gain On Sale—3 Yr	415,000	223,000	9.51%	Annualized IRR—3 Yr	211.13%
Estimated Exit Price/Gain On Sale—5 Yr	450,000	258,000	9.48%	Annualized IRR—5 Yr	148.68%

Table 6.7 Refinance Analyzer

Maximum Refinance—Cash Out			Key Ratios	
Max Refinance	80.00%	304,720	Total Square Feet	2,400.000
Owner's Equity @	20.00%	76,180	Avg Sq Ft/Unit	2,400.000
Required Appraisal	100.00%	380,900	Avg Rent/Sq Ft	1.333
			Avg Cost/Sq Ft	158.708
	Annual	Monthly	Avg Unit Cost	380,899.651
Interest Rate	7.500%	0.625%	Capitalization Rate	9.577%
Amortization Period	25	300	Gross Rent Multiplier	9.919
Payment	27,022	2,252	Expense/Unit	0.000
			Expense/Foot	0.000

Operating Revenues		Year 1
Gross Scheduled Income		38,400
Vacancy rate		1,920
Net Rental Income		36,480
Other Income		0
Gross Revenues	100.0%	36,480

Refinance Matrix	
Max Refinance	CF/DS
411,372	100.0%
403,306	102.0%
395,550	104.0%
388,086	106.0%
380,900	108.0%

Operating Expenses		
Repairs and Maintenance	0.0%	0
Property Management Fees	0.0%	0
Taxes	0.0%	0
Insurance	0.0%	0
Salaries and Wages	0.0%	0
Utilities	0.0%	0
Trash Removal	0.0%	0
Professional Fees	0.0%	0
Advertising	0.0%	0
Other	0.0%	0
Total Op. Exp.	0.0%	0

Refinance Matrix cont.	
373,974	110.0%
367,296	112.0%
360,852	114.0%
354,631	116.0%
348,620	118.0%
342,810	120.0%
337,190	122.0%
331,751	124.0%
326,485	126.0%
321,384	128.0%
316,440	130.0%
311,645	132.0%

Net Operation Income	100.0%	36,480
Dep. Exp.—Building		4,182
Dep. Exp.—Equip.		0
Net Income Before Taxes		32,298
Income Tax Rate	0.0%	0
Net Income After Taxes		32,298

Refinance Matrix cont.	
306,994	134.0%
302,479	136.0%
298,095	138.0%
293,837	140.0%
289,698	142.0%
285,675	144.0%
281,761	146.0%
277,954	148.0%
274,248	150.0%
270,639	152.0%

Cash Flow From Operations		
Net Income After Taxes		32,298
Dep. Exp.		4,182
Total Cash Available for Loan Servicing		36,480
Debt Service		27,022
Remaining After Tax CF From Ops		9,458
Plus Principal Reduction		4,315
Total Return		13,772
CF/Debt Servicing Ratio		135.0%

Refinance Matrix cont.	
267,124	154.0%
263,700	156.0%
260,362	158.0%
257,107	160.0%
253,933	162.0%
250,836	164.0%
247,814	166.0%
244,864	168.0%
241,983	170.0%
239,170	172.0%

difference of \$131,920. This is another powerful example of the effectiveness of the value play strategy. We have taken an existing property and increased its value substantially by changing its use from residential to commercial. The ROI on our original investment, if sold using the assumptions in Table 6.5 is a phenomenal 1,005 percent.

Return on investment (ROI)

$$= \frac{\text{profit margin}}{\text{primary down payment} + \text{secondary down payment}}$$

$$= \frac{\$193,000}{\$19,200} = 1,005.21\%$$

By now you should have a good understanding of the different valuation approaches and their proper application. We have analyzed in depth three real-life examples of how these approaches can be applied. We have examined (1) a residential property using the comparable sales approach, (2) 22 duplex units that were sold based on the comparable sales approach rather than the income approach, and (3) a residential property that was converted to an income property and valued using the income approach. A comprehensive understanding of these valuation methodologies is vitally important to your success in this business.

Firmness of purpose is one of the most necessary sinews of character, and one of the best instruments of success. Without it genius wastes its efforts in a maze of inconsistencies.

—*Lord Chesterfield*

Chapter 7

Seven Steps of Successful Negotiations

In Chapter 5, we examined the three most commonly used approaches for appraising real estate and determined that the comparable sales method was the most appropriate approach to use for single-family houses. In Chapter 6, we studied three examples showing how to apply those approaches to real-world transactions. In this chapter, we examine seven techniques that will enable you to negotiate the best possible price and terms for the purchase of a property. (See Exhibit 7.1.) As you will discover over time, many of the buyers and sellers with whom you negotiate are amateurs, meaning that they do not buy or sell real estate with any degree of frequency. They participate in the market out of necessity. Professional real estate investors, on the other hand, have mastered the seven steps of successful negotiations and use them to their advantage at every opportunity.

THE PSYCHOLOGY OF NEGOTIATING

One of the most important things to remember when negotiating with others is that you are dealing with people, many of whom develop an emotional attachment somewhere in the process. Most

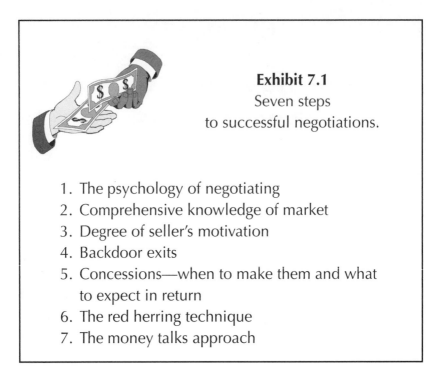

Exhibit 7.1
Seven steps
to successful negotiations.

1. The psychology of negotiating
2. Comprehensive knowledge of market
3. Degree of seller's motivation
4. Backdoor exits
5. Concessions—when to make them and what to expect in return
6. The red herring technique
7. The money talks approach

of the buyers and sellers you deal with are not professionals and often find it difficult to separate their emotions from the rational aspects required to conduct business. After a certain point in the process, people become emotionally engaged, which causes them to act in a manner they otherwise wouldn't. This is especially true for sellers.

For example, an individual who has had his property listed for sale for several months begins to worry about whether his house will ever sell. Then one day a buyer comes along who expresses a sincere interest in the house. Mr. Seller begins to think there is hope, after all. His real estate agents suggests that an offer might be forthcoming. Mr. Seller becomes eager with anticipation at the thought that he can sell his house and move on with his plans. He thinks about all the things he can do with the money he will make from the sale—the new car, paying off some old debts, and buying a nice gift for his wife. Just as Ms. Buyer is getting ready to make an offer, she discovers another house that she likes better and buys it instead. Feelings of despair immediately set in with Mr. Seller. There go all of his hopes and dreams, for once again it seems as if he will never sell his house.

I recall one time when I was negotiating for a tract of land in a prime location. The sellers were two older gentlemen who had owned the land for a number of years. They were asking $400,000 for the land. I had expressed a strong interest in the property and had preliminary discussions with the sellers indirectly, through a broker. The time came for all of us to sit down at the table to work out the details. I thought the property was priced too high relative to other tracts of land in the area and felt a more reasonable price was closer to $350,000. The two gentlemen, who were brothers, were well into their retirement years. It was apparent to me that one of the brothers was very eager to sell and was willing to consider the lower price. Sitting across the table from them, it was easy to read their facial expressions. The brother willing to consider the lower price was practically salivating with anticipation at the thought of cashing out. My guess is that in his mind, he perhaps had visions of being out on the water off the coast of Florida in his new boat. Had I been negotiating only with him, the $350,000 price would easily have been achieved. Unfortunately, his brother was not as eager to sell and held out for close to full asking price. I decided that the deal was overpriced and indicated my unwillingness to proceed. The brother who had visions of retirement was crestfallen as I announced my decision to terminate the negotiations.

Remember that at some point in the negotiating process, the parties you are dealing with will most likely become emotionally engaged. Once they do, it is difficult for them to turn back. In their mind, the property is sold and they are already spending the money. As a professional, you should watch closely for signals sent by the other party's facial expressions and body language. Use these subtle, yet very real, signals to negotiate the best price and terms possible.

COMPREHENSIVE KNOWLEDGE OF MARKET

To be successful in this business, you must have a comprehensive knowledge of your market. It is impossible to negotiate for the best price without it. You must understand property values in your respective market as well as, or better than, the parties with whom you are conducting business. You can use your knowledge to make sound arguments that support the price and terms you are negotiating for. By showing the other parties what similar properties are selling for, you present reasonable and logical data that will help convince them of your position.

I am very familiar with both housing prices and land prices in my particular market and therefore am better prepared to negotiate for the best possible price. One example that comes to mind centers around several vacant lots in a new residential community that a developer had available for sale. His initial asking price was $46,000 per lot. My research indicated that although a number of lots were for sale at $46,000 (and even more), this seller's lots were considerably smaller. The lots selling for $46,000 in that area typically ranged in size from a third to a half of an acre, and some included other features such as trees or a site that would accommodate a walkout basement. The lots I was considering were much smaller in size, probably no more than a fifth of an acre, and had no trees. Since I had done my homework and was familiar with the market, I knew that comparable lots in another new community within a mile of this one were selling for $35,000 to $37,500. I presented this information, complete with the community plat plans, lot sizes, and prices, to the seller to make a valid argument for a lower price. We eventually settled on a price of $36,000 per lot, $10,000 less than his initial asking price.

As Symphony Homes is a residential builder in a very competitive marketplace, it is imperative that we control costs through each and every step of the building process, beginning with the acquisition of land. If I had agreed to pay the extra $10,000 per lot the seller was asking, I would have been at an immediate disadvantage compared to other sellers in the area. To compensate for the difference in price, I would have had to do one of two things—raise the price of the house by $10,000 or absorb the cost within the company. Raising the price would have meant the turnover time for each house sold would increase significantly, which adds directly to carrying costs such as interest, taxes, and insurance. Absorbing a cost of $10,000 per house is not feasible, either, as it would quickly put our company out of business. Although I really liked the lots being offered for sale, had the seller not conceded, we would not have had a deal. I have enough experience to know that there is always another opportunity just around the corner. To overpay for a particular property just because you have fallen in love with it or have become emotionally engaged would border on suicide for your company.

Whether you are buying vacant lots, single-family houses, or apartment buildings, you cannot afford to overpay for a piece of property. As a professional real estate investor, you must be intimately familiar with the market in which you are dealing. Only by possessing a comprehensive knowledge of it can you be truly successful. Without this key information, you will soon discover that you cannot survive in the business of buying and selling real estate.

DEGREE OF SELLER'S MOTIVATION

As a professional real estate investor, it is important for you to know why a particular seller is selling a property. Knowing the underlying reasons for the sale can potentially give you an advantage during the negotiation process. For example, you want to know if the seller has just lost a job and can no longer afford the payments or is perhaps simply testing the market to see how much the property is worth. In other words, you want to know if your seller is a motivated seller and, if so, to what degree. The more motivated the seller, the more likely he or she will be flexible on both price and terms. While there are many reasons for selling, they typically fall into one or more of the seven categories shown in Exhibit 7.2.

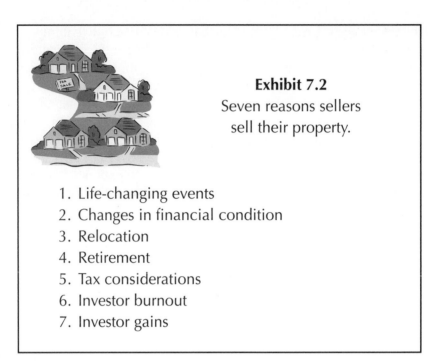

Exhibit 7.2
Seven reasons sellers
sell their property.

1. Life-changing events
2. Changes in financial condition
3. Relocation
4. Retirement
5. Tax considerations
6. Investor burnout
7. Investor gains

The primary reason that sellers sell their properties is because of *life-changing events.* Life-changing events include such things as marriage, the birth of a baby, divorce, illness in the family, accident, or death of a loved one. These types of events are what I refer to as *high-degree motivators* meaning that one or more family members are highly motivated to sell their house. They need and want to do so quickly and are unlikely to hold out for top dollar. The sellers who are affected by these circumstances often have a very real and immediate need to sell and are therefore more likely to be flexible about both price and terms. Life-changing events often create an urgent need to sell, which outweighs the need to profit from the transaction.

Going through a divorce, for example, often creates a financial hardship for the family, especially in a more traditional household in which the father is the provider and the mother is the primary caregiver to the children. In such a situation, all members of the family are affected. Where one larger house was adequate before, two smaller houses or apartments will be necessary now.

Another reason sellers sell their properties is directly related to *changes in their financial condition.* These changes may also be a high-degree motivator, depending on the degree of financial change. The most likely cause of financial hardship is a change in employment circumstances. The seller may have been caught in the latest round of downsizing or right-sizing or whatever the current buzzword may be. The bottom line is that the seller is now unemployed and therefore no longer able to meet his or her financial obligations. Changes in a seller's financial condition may also be a result of a life-changing event, as previously discussed.

Relocation is a third reason for selling property. It is not at all uncommon for an individuals to be required by employers to move to another area for one reason or another. Sometimes the employee knows well in advance of the impending move and has plenty of time to plan and prepare. Other times, however, the employee is given very little notice and must price the house for a quick sale. Some employers actually compensate their employees for moving expenses and also offer to purchase the house at market value if it does not sell. This, however, is the exception rather than the rule. The majority of employers give their employees a choice of absorbing these costs (if they want to keep their jobs) or being terminated.

Another reason for selling is *retirement.* Everyone reaches a point in life at which they are ready to retire. With the aging baby boomers, more people than ever are retiring. Several years ago, I purchased a 25-unit apartment building from an older couple who had reached retirement age. Ironically, the couple had owned the apartment complex for exactly 25 years and had just made their very last mortgage payment. Selling the apartments would provide them with a considerable lump sum of cash that would allow them to more comfortably retire.

Another reason for selling property might be the *tax considerations* of the seller. For example, if someone is selling investment property such as rental units or commercial space and is also involved in an exchange of like properties, then that person is limited by law to a predetermined number of days to close on another investment property. These strict time constraints can impact the seller on both ends of the transaction, meaning the property being sold and also the one being acquired. A seller who has not yet identified a new property to purchase may not be motivated to sell—and may in fact stall the sale of his or her property. On the other hand, a seller who has identified another property that must soon be closed on due to the expiration of that seller's time must be prepared to rapidly strike a deal with a buyer of his or her property.

Investor burnout is another primary reason people sell their houses. They excitedly purchase their first few rental houses with the notion that at last they have made it. Then reality sets in. The tenants call complaining about the broken air conditioner or the dishwasher that needs replacing. Then there's Uncle Joe who just died and your tenants have to help Aunt Sally with the funeral expenses, so they don't have this month's rent. I've heard enough excuses in my experience to fill a book. I remember one lady who did everything she could to avoid paying her rent. On one occasion, she stopped by our office to pay her rent on her way to work, so she was in a hurry. In the blink of an eye, she dropped off a check and was out the door. "Thank you," I called out to her as she whisked away. The amount of rent due from this lady was $575.00. I vividly remember glancing down at the check and feeling my anger rise as I realized the amount of the check she wrote was $5.75, not $575.00! Since I knew she worked right down the street, I quickly hopped in my car and confronted her about the error. She acted surprised by her "oversight," but I think she was more surprised by the fact that I caught up with her than anything else. She wrote another check on the spot, this time for the correct amount. In the case of investor burnout, the degree of the seller's motivation will correlate directly with the degree of distress. This is where subtle clues can be detected by direct communication with the seller. If the seller is suffering from burnout related to managing his or her property, that person will most likely be highly motivated, and a highly motivated seller is a flexible seller.

Finally, one of the most compelling reasons for sellers to divest themselves of property is for *investor gains.* Value players like yourself are ready to take their gains on the sale and move on to the next value play opportunity. The degree of motivation will vary depending on factors such as how much value was created in the deal and timing for entry into the next investment. If, for example, sellers have identified another retail opportunity but need the cash out of their current house, then they may be willing to strike a bargain, knowing that they will make up for it, and then some, on the next transaction. Investors buying and selling in volume are not interested in holding out for top dollar. They prefer to take a little less and keep their turnover high, knowing that the more houses they buy and sell, the more financially rewarding it will be.

As you work with and talk to sellers, ask them why they are selling. Listen both to what they do tell you and to what they don't tell you. Sometimes they will be very direct, as in, "My wife and I just got a divorce." Other times, however, you must watch and listen for subtle clues about their true reason for selling. They may tell you, for example, that they are retiring, but leave out the part about having already purchased a condo in Florida that's forcing them to make two payments and really beginning to stretch the budget and "Oh, if we could only sell this house we could move to Florida." A little probing can often uncover the seller's underlying motives to sell.

BACKDOOR EXITS

Backdoor exits, or *escape clauses* as they are also referred to, allow you to back out of a purchase agreement at various times throughout the contract period. You should always take care to ensure that several escape clauses are built into the contract, with at least one of these clauses giving you the right to back out right up to the point of closing. The proper application of these techniques can provide the shrewd investor with tremendous bargaining power.

A contingency is a common backdoor exit used by many investors. The types of contingencies are limited only by your imagination. Some examples include "contingent upon purchaser selling her residence" and "contingent upon seller making repairs prior to closing as indicated in Addendum A." There are also many provisions and conditions that must be satisfied before the purchaser's earnest money "goes hard," or becomes nonrefundable. You can easily protect yourself with a provision such as "subject to satisfactory inspection of the property and acceptance thereof by purchaser." Typically, you have anywhere from 14 to 30 days to accept the property based on its physical condition. The number of days is usually a fill-in-the-blank type of provision, so you can ask for more time if necessary. The seller may not give you more time, but it doesn't hurt to ask. In some instances, approvals may be required by state and local authorities. For example, if there is a change in use of the property from residential to commercial, the city board of zoning appeals must review and subsequently approve the change. You certainly want to include language in the agreement that will fully protect you in the event that the approvals are not granted.

One of my favorite techniques is a very simple, yet powerful, backdoor exit. On the first page of most purchase agreements are several paragraphs outlining the financing provisions. Buyers are given the right to obtain suitable financing within a certain number of days of signing the agreement. They usually have anywhere from 3 to 7 days to apply for financing and 7 to 14 days to obtain an approval. Since most sellers assume they are working with a buyer who is fully qualified and will be approved for the required financing, this section of the purchase agreement is often glossed over. Throughout the standardized purchase agreements most often used, there are ample opportunities to fill in the blanks. Under the financing provisions section, there is almost always a blank to fill in for the interest rate not to exceed a certain amount and also one for the loan-to-value percentage. Here is where you protect yourself in not one, but two places. If you know that the prevailing market interest rate for loans is 6.5 percent, for example, you fill in the blank with

6.0 percent. Since it is not at all uncommon for buyers to get 95 percent loans, and even 97 percent loans, on houses they purchase, you fill in the blank with 95 percent. You comply with the time requirements as outlined in the financing section, but as a real estate professional buying investment property, you will most likely be able to get a loan for only up to 90 percent of the value. When your approval comes back from the lender offering an interest rate of 6.6 percent and a loan-to-value ratio of 90 percent, the seller believes that you have been approved. While it is true that you have in fact been approved, you have not been approved under the terms and conditions as set forth in the purchase agreement. You can use this very simple, but very powerful, technique as a backdoor exit on almost any property you enter into a contract on, right up to the very last minute. The seller won't like it one bit, but it is a very real legal out for you.

CONCESSIONS

Concessions can be another very effective method of getting exactly what you want during the negotiation phase. My approach is initially to ask for more than I expect to get. For example, I may ask sellers to accept a price substantially below the asking price, to include all of the appliances, to carry back a second mortgage for 15 percent of the deal value, to allow an additional credit at closing for repairs, and to pay for all of the closing costs. I know going in that I will most likely not get all of what I ask for, but then again, you never know. Sellers may be just anxious enough to agree to everything you ask for. On the other hand, they may instead present a counteroffer to partially reduce the price, pay for the closing costs, and give you a credit for repairs, but not carry back a second mortgage or include the appliances. In counteroffering, the sellers may make several concessions, which you can then decide whether to accept.

Concessions can also be used as a kind of bargaining chip. You tell the seller, "I will agree to X if you will agree to Y." One example of this kind of bargaining is an agreement to pay the seller's full asking price if he in turn agrees to accept only 5 percent down instead of the 20 percent originally desired. Another example is a seller who must have all cash and is pushing for a quick closing. You agree to her request, but only if she concedes to accept $10,000 less than the asking price. Concessions are most effectively used to gain something in your favor related to the transaction in exchange for something else.

THE RED HERRING TECHNIQUE

One of my favorite negotiating methods is one I refer to as "the red herring technique." The phrase can be traced back to the practice of escaped convicts who used pickled herring to throw bloodhounds off their scent. In essence, the red herring technique creates a distraction that is completely irrelevant to the subject at hand. As a professional real estate investor, you can use this technique to create a distraction from the real issue you are negotiating. The technique works like this. Let's say the seller is asking $90,000 for his house and that he wants all cash. You inspect the property and determine that although the asking price appears to be fair, you are going to make a concerted effort to purchase it for 10 percent below market value. During the course of your inspection, you happen to notice stored in the garage a pair of prized Yamaha WaveRunners. You decide to write an offer structured as follows:

- Sales price of $81,000
- Seller to carry back a second mortgage for $10,000
- Seller to include two Yamaha WaveRunners
- Seller to pay for all closing costs

Now then, can you guess which provision is the red herring? Of course you can! It's the inclusion of the pair of WaveRunners! Can you imagine how the seller will react when your offer is presented to him? He's likely to breeze right past everything with the exception of the WaveRunners. He'll probably say something like, "What's this? Include my WaveRunners? That buyer must be crazy! There's no way he's getting my WaveRunners!" Meanwhile, he signs off on everything else, but he absolutely refuses to include those WaveRunners. You, of course, didn't care about them to begin with. Your objective was to get your price and terms by creating a distraction that had nothing at all to do with the original transaction.

I recently used this technique to shave $5,000 off of an already below-market asking price. We named our company Symphony Homes because we have an interest in most anything related to music, especially classical music. While inspecting the seller's property, I noticed a very old violin that was carefully mounted on the dining room wall. Because it was so proudly displayed, I figured it had probably been in the seller's family for some time. I wrote the offer for $5,000 less than the seller's asking price. To create a distraction, I wrote in the special provisions section, "Seller to include violin hanging in dining room." I can only imagine the look of surprise as the seller's agent presented the offer to him. The seller countered the very next day. His agent brought the counteroffer to my office and stated rather emphatically on the seller's behalf that there was no way I was getting that violin, as it was a family heirloom. The agent didn't say a word, however, about the lower price. In an effort to mask my true motives, I insisted to the agent that I must have that violin. She reaffirmed the seller's position and again stated that he would not part with it. I finally conceded and signed the counteroffer. The red herring technique is a simple, yet powerfully effective tool in your arsenal of negotiating tactics. Use it wisely to get what you want!

THE MONEY-TALKS APPROACH

The money-talks approach can be an effective negotiation tool to help ensure that more of your offers are accepted. While the approach is simple in its application, the results can be quite powerful. There is a great deal of truth in the phrase "money talks." It works like this. After you have written your offer to include some of the other negotiation techniques previously described, it is time to present it to the seller. When presenting your offer, attach a large check to it to demonstrate to the seller that you are a serious buyer. As a general rule, the check should be written for between 5 and 10 percent of the deal value. This will depend on the housing prices in your particular market, but generally speaking, a check written for at least $5,000 and perhaps up to $25,000 will most certainly get the seller's attention. A large earnest-money deposit sends a strong and immediate signal to the seller that he or she is dealing with a buyer who is both serious and capable of putting together a deal.

Think about it. How many offers have you received where the buyer attached a $500 or $1,000 earnest-money check? Probably three out of four of the offers you receive have minimal deposits attached. When I have a buyer interested in one of my houses show up with a $1,000 deposit, I usually don't get too excited. On the other hand, if someone shows up with a check for 5 to 10 percent of the purchase price, it gets my immediate attention. I once had a buyer who made an offer of $228,000 on a house valued at $235,000. I watch the profit margins pretty closely, so this is a deal that I would normally pass on. In this particular case, however, the buyer attached an earnest-money check in the amount of $12,000. That check immediately got my attention because I knew I was working with a buyer who was both serious and capable of purchasing the house. It took me all of about five minutes to think it over before accepting the offer.

Obtaining the best possible price and terms for the purchase of real estate requires a combination of both art and skill. As a master negotiator, you must take care to exercise each one of the seven steps of successful negotiations discussed in this chapter. To summarize, they are as follows:

1. The psychology of negotiating
2. Comprehensive knowledge of market

3. Degree of seller's motivation
4. Backdoor exits
5. Concessions—when to make them and what to expect in return
6. The red herring technique
7. The money-talks approach

A thorough and comprehensive understanding of each one of these principals can literally save you thousands of dollars on your real estate transactions. The more familiar you become with these principles, the more skilled you will become when negotiating with others.

> You can have anything you want—if you want it badly enough. You can be anything you want to be, do anything you set out to accomplish if you hold to that desire with singleness of purpose.
>
> —*Abraham Lincoln*

Chapter 8

Financing and Closing Considerations

The ability to obtain proper financing for the purchase of your investment property is vital to your success. In this chapter, I examine several financing alternatives available to you and discuss the differences of each. (See Exhibit 8.1.) In addition, I have included a sample outline for a business plan you can use to better prepare yourself when initiating new relationships with lenders or partners. I have also included a section about credit scores and underwriting guidelines. Finally, I provide you with information to better enable you to understand and prepare for the closing process.

CONVENTIONAL MORTGAGES

Conventional mortgages represent an excellent source of financing for your real estate investments. There are a number of loan programs available at any given time that offer a wide range of terms and conditions. Depending on the interest rate environment, conventional mortgage rates can be among the most competitive types of financing. Unlike bank loans, which are usually based on the prime lending rate, mortgage loans are typically based on 10-year T-bills, or Treasury notes, plus some additional spread or

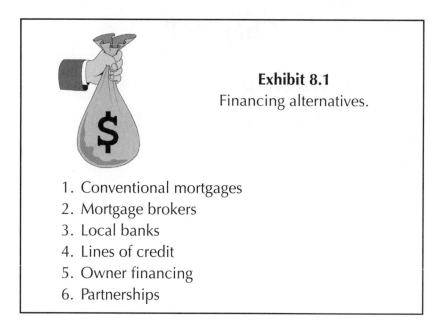

Exhibit 8.1
Financing alternatives.

1. Conventional mortgages
2. Mortgage brokers
3. Local banks
4. Lines of credit
5. Owner financing
6. Partnerships

margin. The result is that conventional mortgage loans generally carry a more favorable interest rate than do other types of financing instruments.

Conventional mortgages are usually available with 30-year amortization periods as well. The longer amortization period helps you to minimize your monthly cash flow requirement to the lender by reducing the amount you must pay back each month. By way of comparison, a loan through your local bank may offer only a 15- or 20-year amortization period. This is not always the case, however, as sometimes interest-only loans are available from a bank. Since no principal payments are being made, the monthly cash flow out can be reduced even further.

Another advantage of using a conventional mortgage company to finance your purchase is that a number of companies will lend up to 90 percent of the purchase price on investment properties. This means you have to come up with only 10 percent for your down payment. For those of you who are accustomed to reading the nothing-down types of books, keep in mind that the selection of available investment opportunities is much narrower. You may spend more time searching for the deal that requires very little down and discover that the upside for creating value and subsequently flipping the property is limited. I prefer to use a little more of my cash and have a much broader selection than to spend time looking for that proverbial needle in a haystack.

While conventional mortgage companies are generally a good source of financing, there are some drawbacks to using them. One such drawback is the documentation required by the lender on each and every transaction. Mortgage companies are notorious for demanding excessive documentation. For example, if a large deposit has recently been made into your bank account, the lender will want documentation to determine its source. Other disadvantages to using a conventional mortgage company are the fees charged for the loan. Depending on the lender, these may or may not include a loan application fee, an underwriting fee, a loan origination fee, and whatever other creative fees the lender can come up with.

MORTGAGE BROKERS

Just as real estate brokers play an important role in matching up buyers and sellers, so do mortgage brokers play an important role in matching up buyers and lenders. Mortgage brokers usually have many contacts in the industry; they know which lender is best suited for the type of financing you are seeking, and they know who's offering the best deal. Experienced brokers have well-established relationships directly with the lenders and usually have two or three with whom they do a large volume of business. While you can generally expect to pay 1 percent to the broker for his or her services, the fee can be well worth it if you are working with a professional broker who has solid relationships with several lenders.

The broker's service can sometimes make the difference in whether the financing for your deal will be accepted. Furthermore, brokers know how to qualify your particular property before ever sending it to a lender because they know what each lender will accept and what they will not accept. Good mortgage brokers can usually tell you if they can place your loan after spending only 10 to 15 minutes with you on the phone. They know what questions to ask to qualify your property and which lender is likely to be the most interested in financing it.

LOCAL BANKS

Conventional bank financing is commonly available through smaller local banks. These types of banks may operate with just a single branch and $15 million in deposits, or they may be somewhat larger with as many as 5 to 10 branches and $150 million in deposits. One advantage of using a local bank is they can often offer borrowers a greater degree of flexibility than other lenders such as mortgage companies. For example, they may provide the money for your rehab improvements, or a percentage thereof, in addition to the financing for the property itself.

Smaller banks are also likely to be much more familiar with the local area and would therefore have a greater degree of confidence in the specific market than would a larger regional or national lender. Personal relationships with your local banker are more easily established than with other types of lenders such as conventional mortgage companies. You can go into the bank, introduce yourself, and sit down and talk directly with the lender. This gives you the opportunity to sell yourself and your project. Once a relationship has been established and the banker gets to know you and is comfortable with you, future loan requests will be much easier and likely require less documentation, possibly as little as updating your personal financial statement.

Local banks are good sources for rehab loans because the lender knows the loans are short term in nature. The banks are also able to generate more fees because of the shorter duration of these types of loans. Local banks may not give you the best terms initially, but the more business you do with them and the more comfortable they become with you, the more leverage you will develop in negotiating more favorable terms with them.

As your relationship with a lender matures, you should seek to establish a predetermined line of credit. This will enable you to borrow money up to your credit limit. For example, with a $1 million line of credit, you will have the ability to purchase several properties at one time. With an average selling price of $100,000 you can effectively purchase up to 10 houses. This depends, of course, on the specific terms the lender has set with respect to the loan-to-value ratio and the collateral required, if any, on each house. Since the lender knows you are in the rehab business, money from your line of credit can usually be used for the repairs also. Again, the lender may limit the percentage of borrowed funds by a predetermined loan-to-value ratio.

LINES OF CREDIT

Several types of credit lines are available to almost anyone. Some of the more common ones are home equity lines of credit, national credit cards like MasterCard and Visa, and individual store credit cards. The terms and conditions vary widely with these types of credit. The most favorable interest rates and the longest terms are typically found with home equity lines of credit, while national credit cards and store credit cards tend to offer higher rates and shorter repayment terms.

Many of you already own your own home. For those who do, you are most likely to be familiar with home equity lines of credit (HELOC) loans. These are merely second mortgages secured by your principal place of residence that allow you to borrow against the equity in your home, oftentimes up to 100 percent of the value of your home, sometimes even more. Since this type of loan is secured by your residence, the interest rates are usually lower than with other types of credit. HELOC loans provide you the flexibility of borrowing against your home at will by simply writing a check. These funds can be used for just about anything you want and represent a good source of funds to be used as down payments and for rehab money.

For those of you who insist on that nothing-down deal, you can easily borrow money against your home equity line of credit and use it for the down payment on an investment property. Since those funds are borrowed funds, they do not represent your cash equity. If, for example, you purchase a house for $85,000 and then borrow $70,000 from your local bank and the remaining $15,000 from your home equity line of credit, you have in essence a nothing-down transaction because 100 percent of the funds used to purchase the house are borrowed funds. You should be aware, however, that this is easier to do with a local bank than with a conventional mortgage lender. Mortgage companies tend to require more documentation and often want to know where the money for your down payment is coming from. You can easily overcome this requirement, however, by depositing the funds at least two months in advance into your bank account. Lenders usually do not require more than the two most current bank statements, and as long as the money is in your account prior to those two periods, the lender will not see the deposit and will therefore not question it. This practice is in no way dishonest. You are simply borrowing money against an approved line of credit and placing the funds into your bank account. The borrowed funds will, however, show up on your credit report and will therefore increase your overall debt-to-income ratio, so if you are already maxed out on credit cards, this may not be the way to go.

National credit cards like MasterCard and Visa also represent a good source of funds. Credit cards are available to almost anyone and can be used for just about anything. Most credit cards offer you the capability of getting a cash advance against your credit limit. You can also write checks that can be used for almost anything, including your investment property. National credit cards tend to carry higher interest rates than do other forms of borrowing, so you should use this source of funds prudently.

Individual store credit cards can provide you with even more buying power. National hardware stores like The Home Depot offer credit cards to their customers enabling them to purchase materials from their stores. If you are in the rehab business, this can be an excellent source of short-term credit that can be used to finance up to 100 percent of the required repairs on your rehab project.

While lines of credit can be a great source of borrowing power, I caution you to use them wisely. Remember that you are using these funds for investment purposes, so be sensible and responsible in the way you use them. Don't go out and max out all of your cards thinking you can conquer the world. Remember that the money has to be repaid at some point in time. Your objective is to earn a predetermined rate of return on all funds borrowed for investment purposes, including the many types of credit lines available to you.

OWNER FINANCING

In an owner financing arrangement, the sellers do exactly as the name implies. They provide the buyer with some form of financing. It may be that they carry the entire note or only a portion thereof. If the sellers own the property free and clear, for example, then they may be willing to provide you with 100 percent financing. More than likely though, the sellers will want a minimal down payment, even if it is only $1,000. If a seller still has a large underlying mortgage on the property, then he or she may be agreeable to carrying back a second mortgage for a smaller amount—10 percent of the purchase price, for example. You will still have to obtain a mortgage for the property from a more traditional source such as a mortgage company, but having the seller carry back a second allows you to get into the deal with less money down. One caveat you should be aware of, though, is that not all lenders will allow a second of any kind to be attached. Before you proceed with this option, make sure the mortgage company does not have a provision in place that would prevent you from attaching a second mortgage to the deal.

There are several advantages of an owner finance arrangement.

One benefit is that the buyer need not conform to all of the underwriting guidelines required of banks and mortgage companies. The seller is likely to require very little in the way of documentation. Unlike conventional mortgage companies, the seller providing owner financing doesn't care where the money for the down payment comes from as long as it comes from somewhere. On the other hand, traditional lenders like banks and mortgage companies can be very particular about where your down payment comes from. In many cases, the money cannot come from a family member or a friend. Moreover, you must be able to prove that the money is your own and did not come from a relative. Another advantage of using owner financing is that it enables you to save a considerable sum by avoiding the fees and transaction costs commonly assessed with new loans. There are no loan application fees, no underwriting fees, and no loan origination fees. Finally, the time needed to close a deal involving owner financing is much less than for traditional financing arrangements since virtually no loan approval process is required.

Another form of owner financing is known as a wraparound mortgage. Under this arrangement, the seller retains title and continues to make mortgage payments to the lender while the new owner makes mortgage payments directly to the seller. Be careful of any due-on-sale clauses in the deed of trust that may expressly prohibit this type of financing arrangement. Lenders normally are not very fond of the transfer of ownership interests without their knowing about it.

Although second-lien positions are the most common form of owner financing arrangements, owners or sellers are not limited to just debt financing. They may be open to an equity agreement wherein they retain a small portion of ownership interest. Instead of being required to make monthly payments to the seller, the buyer and seller agree to share in the profits of the newly formed entity. Depending on the specifics of the agreement, the original seller may also be entitled to a share of any capital gains when the property is later resold.

PARTNERSHIPS

Using the resources of a partner can be an excellent form of secondary financing. The type of partner I am referring to in this section is a friend, family member, or business acquaintance. Partnerships can be structured in any number of ways. For instance, capital injections by partners can take the form of debt or equity, partners can play an active or passive role, and terms for the repayment provisions can be defined in various creative ways.

If your partner agrees to invest in your project using equity, then he or she will share the risk with you. If you lose, your partner loses, but if you win, your partner also wins and shares in the profits. On the other hand, if you don't want to give up any of your profits, then you would have your partner participate on the debt side by making a loan to you. In this case, the loan can be secured by the property or by any other collateral you may have, or it may be an unsecured loan as well. You may decide to have your partners actively participate by using whatever skill sets they may have. Partners who are mechanically inclined, for example, may be able to perform some of the maintenance. Conversely, you may choose to have partners play a passive role wherein their only function is to provide capital. Repayment provisions can be made in any number of ways. For example, debt payments can be made periodically (e.g., monthly, quarterly, or annually). You might also agree to repay the debt with all interest due when the property is sold. If, on the other hand, you are flipping several properties a year, it may not make sense to repay the debt when the first property is sold. You will likely want to have your partner agree to an ongoing arrangement that provides you the flexibility to buy and sell at will with a predetermined repayment date agreed to by both parties. In summary, allowing a partner to participate can benefit you by providing additional capital for a project that otherwise may have been out of reach and by contributing services or specific skills that you may be lacking.

YOUR BUSINESS PLAN

Preparing a professional-looking, comprehensive business plan and presenting it to potential lenders and partners is certain to set you apart from the dozens of applicants they meet day in and day out. Preparing a business plan will also compel you to clearly define your real estate investment objectives. Physically going through the motions of formalizing your business plan forces you to think through each and every step of the process and subsequently assess the soundness of your plan. Your vision of where and how you want to grow your company begins in your mind with your thought processes. Recording your thoughts in a formalized manner allows you to crystallize them. You can refer to your business plan as often as needed to make sure you are on track to reach your objectives and also to adjust your course as necessary.

Furthermore, presenting your business plan directly to potential lenders or partners demonstrates that you are a serious investor who is looking to establish a long-term relationship. By following the step-by-step process outlined in your business plan, potential lenders will also be able to judge the soundness of your plan. In short, it will enable them to establish a level of comfort with you and your transaction that may not otherwise be possible. You must remember that prospective lenders and partners are human beings who will judge you not only by what they see on your loan application, but also by what they see in the way you present yourself to them. You must be prepared to sell yourself and your abilities to them. Their assessment of you is based on both objective evidence and subjective qualities they observe about you. The objective evidence is drawn from the items that are in black and white before them, such as your loan application and credit scores. The subjective qualities you will be judged on are more subtle in nature and include such things as the way you present yourself, your level of professionalism, and whether they perceive you to be credible.

The use of a sound business plan is most effective when dealing with local banks or partners. These are the people you are most likely to get to know on a more personal level. A business plan is of little or no value to mortgage brokers, since they are more interested in packaging your loan request and shipping it off to any one of many underwriting departments. Although formalizing your business plan will require a good deal of time and effort on your part, a comprehensive and professional-looking plan can pay big dividends by providing you with the much needed capital to fund your purchases.

Exhibit 8.2 provides a sample outline for some of the more essential items you will want to include in your business plan. These items can be organized in a very professional manner in a notebook that contains tabs and dividers.

WHAT EVERY BORROWER SHOULD KNOW ABOUT CREDIT SCORES

Most lenders today use what is known as FICO scores to determine your ability to borrow money and repay a loan. FICO is an acronym for Fair, Isaac, and Company, which uses an elaborate model to calculate data collected over a period of time about specific individuals. This historical data is then used to assign a credit score to that individual. The scoring system uses factors such as payment history, number of creditors, debt-to-income ratios, outstanding balances relative to credit limits, length of credit history, types of credit, and reported income. Before the final score is calculated, previously established weights are assigned to each variable according to the criteria set forth in the model. When lenders order your credit history, they typically get it from all three of the following sources: Equifax, Experian, and TransUnion. All three services may not have exactly the same information, so the credit scores may vary among them. Lenders often use either an average of the three scores or the median score.

The credit score range is from 300 to 850, with 300 being extremely poor and 850 being a perfect score. It is highly recommended that you do everything within your power to maintain as

Exhibit 8.2
Components of an
effective business plan.

1. *Executive summary.* A one- or two-page summary of your plan.
2. *Company profile.* Background information about yourself, including experience and education, and information about your company.
3. *Financial statements.* Personal and company financials.
4. *Primary market.* Define your intended market area.
5. *Business strategy.* Provide in detail your specific short-term and long-term objectives for your company.
6. *Marketing strategy.* Define your target market and include specifics of how you intend to market your services and/or properties.
7. *Capital requirements.* List short-term and long-term anticipated capital requirements.
8. *Financial analysis.* Provide supporting financial tables.
9. *Summary.* Summarize your proposal and close with sound reasons about why the lender or partner should work with you.
10. *Exhibits.* May include photographs, surveys, tax returns, purchase agreements, addendums, and so on.

high a score as possible. If your score is 700+, you are considered to be an A borrower and will have no problem qualifying for a loan, provided you meet whatever other criteria the lender has set forth.

Credit scores are used much like scholastic aptitude test (SAT) or graduate management admission test (GMAT) scores. The first thing university administrators want to know when students apply for entrance is how well they did on the required standardized tests. The tests are used to measure students' knowledge and aptitude in various subjects and the results are quantitatively summarized in the form of a numeric score. Just as administrators use these scores to set minimum standards for matriculation into their schools, so do lenders use credit scores to set minimum standards for loaning money to prospective borrowers. Credit scores serve as a valuable tool to lenders because they are purely objective in measuring the ability of a borrower to repay a loan and the probability that he or she will default. They remove all elements of subjective judgment that could be considered discriminatory, such as race or religious preferences.

Some lenders will make loans to just about anyone. They don't care what your score is as long as the property is generating adequate income to service the debt. These lenders will, however, adjust their interest rates accordingly by applying a matrix grid that matches your ability to repay with the condition of the property. You can see by looking at Table 8.1 that borrowers who fail to maintain good credit are usually penalized as a result. The logic

Table 8.1 Interest Rate Matrix

Property Rating	Borrower Rating			
	A	B	C	D
A	6.00%	6.50%	7.00%	7.50%
B	6.50%	7.00%	7.50%	8.00%
C	7.00%	7.50%	8.00%	8.50%
D	7.50%	8.00%	8.50%	9.00%

is quite simple. Lenders charge a higher rate of interest to offset the higher risk associated with borrowers who have poor credit. The bottom line to you as an investor is to work hard to maintain the best credit rating possible. Doing so will enable you to borrow money more easily than those who have poor credit—and also at much more favorable terms and conditions.

UNDERWRITING GUIDELINES

All lenders have established criteria for making loan decisions. These criteria are referred to as the lender's *underwriting guidelines*. These guidelines form the basis for all decisions made to either approve or decline a loan applicant's request. They represent the lender's policies and procedures to which all new loans under review must conform before being granted final approval. A lender's underwriting guidelines may include elements such as the loan-to-value (LTV) ratio, the debt service coverage ratio (DSCR), a borrower's debt-to-income ratio, the size and term of the loan, and information about the subject property.

To assure that its underwriting guidelines are conformed to, a lender will require specific information about the property and the borrower in order to do a full and proper analysis of a loan request. This information includes items such as the purchase agreement for the property, credit reports from no fewer than three independent agencies, verification of employment and income, bank statements, and tax returns. See Exhibit 8.3 for a more complete list. Providing the lender with a complete documentation package enables it to expedite the processing of your loan in a timely and efficient manner. Once the lender has all the necessary documentation, you can usually have an approval within two or three days. This is, however, a general time frame and may vary depending on the volume of loans being processed at any given time. Oftentimes the underwriter will come back and ask for more information, primarily to clarify something you have already submitted. For example, if your bank statement shows an unusually large deposit being made into your account, the underwriter is likely to require supporting documentation about the source of those funds.

You should be aware that smaller local banks are usually not as sticky about requiring you to document the source of funds. Banks customarily require only the first page of your account statement to document the amount of funds you have and not necessarily their source. You can use this to your advantage if you wish to deposit borrowed funds, such as those from a home equity loan or a credit card. Making a deposit of this sort does not mean you are being dishonest or breaking any laws. Unless the bank

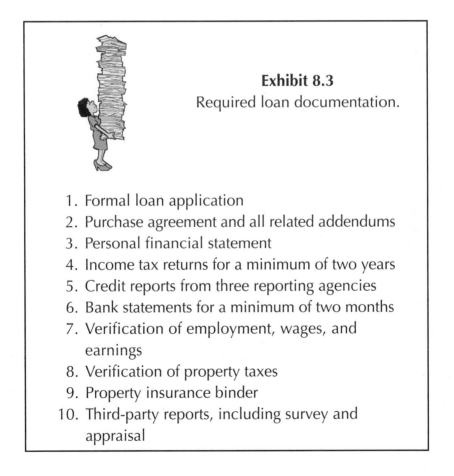

Exhibit 8.3
Required loan documentation.

1. Formal loan application
2. Purchase agreement and all related addendums
3. Personal financial statement
4. Income tax returns for a minimum of two years
5. Credit reports from three reporting agencies
6. Bank statements for a minimum of two months
7. Verification of employment, wages, and earnings
8. Verification of property taxes
9. Property insurance binder
10. Third-party reports, including survey and appraisal

asks you specifically about the source of the deposit, you are not required to disclose it to them. Even if your bank asks, local banks are often not as particular about your using borrowed money (e.g., from a home equity line of credit) as a conventional mortgage company might be.

After securing financing for your property, the next step is to begin preparing to finalize and close the transaction. Depending on the size of your acquisition, the closing process can be fairly simple and straightforward, or it can be quite involved, with extensive documentation required. It is also time to begin planning and defining your role as a strategic manager. This, too, will depend on the size of the transaction and your level of experience.

THE CLOSING PROCESS

The closing process is the point in time when everything comes together to finalize your transaction. You have studied the market and analyzed numerous investment opportunities; you have successfully negotiated terms and conditions acceptable to both you and the seller; and you have sought out the best financing alternative for your property. It is now time to bring all the parties together to close the sale. Before you commit yourself by signing on the dotted line, however, you should take time to thoroughly review all related closing documents—in particular, the title report, closing statement, deed of trust, and promissory note.

The *title report,* also known as the *abstract of title,* provides information about the property's chain of title. In other words, it gives a history of ownership, judgments, liens, and anything else that may have been recorded against the property over time. The title insurance company issues an insurance policy to the buyer and a separate policy to the lender. These guarantee the title is clean and that there are no encumbrances that may adversely affect the new owner.

Closing statements, also known as *settlement statements,* are commonly prepared by the title company handling the closing.

They detail by line item all associated debits and credits assessed to both buyer and seller. These include such items as the sale price, amount of earnest money deposit, principal amount of the new loan, any existing loans or debts that must be satisfied, pro-rated adjustments for taxes and interest, and various fees charged by the title company. Tables 8.2 through 8.5 collectively provide you with some of the detail from a commonly used closing settlement statement form.

You should take the requisite time to review each and every charge on the settlement statement to verify its accuracy. Errors are often inadvertently made for one reason or another. The title company may, for example, have the incorrect payoff amount of the seller's loan or may calculate the prorations incorrectly or may not be aware of a credit you are entitled to because of a specific clause in the purchase agreement negotiated by you and the seller. Don't assume that because closing officers work at title companies and act as facilitators in numerous closings that "they must be right because they are closers and they should know." Precisely the opposite is true. Because closers do act as facilitators in numerous closings each and every day is all the more reason they must rely on you to provide accurate information for the settlement statement.

Neglecting to review the closing statement can be very risky and potentially cost you hundreds or even thousands of dollars. Here in Michigan, for example, the state and county assess what is referred to as a *transfer tax*. The transfer tax is calculated as a percentage of the sales price and is collected at closing on all real estate sold. It is just like paying tax on a new car, new furniture, school supplies for the kids, or just about anything else Uncle Sam can get his hands on. The tax rate applied is usually about 1 percent or just a little less, so for every $100,000 in property value sold, approximately $1,000 in taxes is assessed. Unless otherwise stated, the seller is responsible for paying this tax. In my purchase agreements, however, I require the buyer to pay the tax. Unless the title company has been made aware of this, the transfer taxes will be placed, incorrectly, on my side of the settlement statement. This error, which has been made many times, could easily cost me $2,000 to $3,000.

Table 8.2   Settlement Statement

U.S. Department of Housing and Urban Development			OMB No. 2502-0265

B. Type of Loan

1. ☐ FHA   2. ☐ FmHA   3. ☐ Conv. Unins.
4. ☐ VA   5. ☒ Conv. Ins.

6. File Number	7. Loan Number	8. Mortgage Insurance Case Number

C. NOTE: *This form is furnished to give you a statement of actual settlement costs. Amounts paid to and by the settlement agent are shown. Items marked "(p.o.c.)" were paid outside the closing; they are shown here for informational purposes and are not included in the totals.*

D. NAME OF BORROWER:
ADDRESS OF BORROWER:

E. NAME OF SELLER: Symphony Homes Real Estate Group, L.L.C.
ADDRESS OF SELLER:

F. NAME OF LENDER:
ADDRESS OF LENDER:

G. PROPERTY LOCATION: Davison, Genesee County, Michigan 48433

H. SETTLEMENT AGENT:
PLACE OF SETTLEMENT:

I. SETTLEMENT DATE: 10/30/2002   **PRORATION DATE: 10/30/2002**

J.	SUMMARY OF BORROWER'S TRANSACTION		K.	SUMMARY OF SELLER'S TRANSACTION	
100. GROSS AMOUNT DUE FROM BORROWER:			**400. GROSS AMOUNT DUE TO SELLER:**		
101. Contract sale price		42,000.00	401. Contract sale price		42,000.00
102. Personal property		167,700.00	402. Personal property		167,700.00
103. Settlement charges to borrower *(from line 1400)*		5,234.28	403.		
104.			404.		
105.			405.		
ADJUSTMENTS FOR ITEMS PAID BY SELLER IN ADVANCE:			**ADJUSTMENTS FOR ITEMS PAID BY SELLER IN ADVANCE:**		
106. City\Town taxes 10/30/2002 to 07/01/2003		12.11	406. City\Town taxes 10/30/2002 to 07/01/2003		12.11
107. County taxes 10/30/2002 to 01/01/2003		5.70	407. County taxes 10/30/2002 to 01/01/2003		5.70
108. Assessments to			408. Assessments to		
109. Condo Dues Pro-Rata 10/30/02-12/31/02		17.01	409. Condo Dues Pro-Rata 10/30/02-12/31/02		17.01
110.			410.		
111.			411.		
112.			412.		
120. GROSS AMOUNT DUE FROM BORROWER: >>		**214,969.10**	**420. GROSS AMOUNT DUE TO SELLER:** >>		**209,734.82**
200. AMOUNTS PAID BY OR IN BEHALF OF BORROWER:			**500. REDUCTIONS IN AMOUNT DUE TO SELLER:**		
201. Deposit or earnest money		10,600.00	501. Excess deposit (see *instructions*)		10,600.00
202. Principal amount of new loan(s)		199,215.00	502. Settlement charges to seller *(line 1400)*		6,350.00
203. Existing loan(s) taken subject to			503. Existing loan(s) taken subject to		
204.			504. Payoff of first mortgage loan Payoff Ln.		153,316.56
205.			505. Payoff of second mortgage loan		
206.			506. Sewer & Water Due 11/5/02		14.02
207.			507. Sewer & Water Escrow		75.00
208.			508.		
209.			509.		
ADJUSTMENTS FOR ITEMS UNPAID BY SELLER:			**ADJUSTMENTS FOR ITEMS UNPAID BY SELLER:**		
210. City\Town taxes to			510. City\Town taxes to		
211. County taxes to			511. County taxes to		
212. Assessments to			512. Assessments to		
213.			513.		
214.			514.		
215.			515.		
216.			516.		
217.			517.		
218.			518.		
219.			519.		
220. TOTAL PAID BY\FOR BORROWER: >>		**209,815.00**	**520. TOTAL REDUCTIONS IN AMOUNT DUE SELLER:** >>		**170,355.58**
300. CASH AT SETTLEMENT FROM\TO BORROWER:			**600. CASH AT SETTLEMENT TO\FROM SELLER:**		
301. Gross amount due from borrower *(line 120)*		214,969.10	601. Gross amount due to seller *(line 420)*		209,734.82
302. Less amount paid by\for borrower *(line 220)*		209,815.00	602. Less total reductions in amount due seller *(line 520)*		170,355.58
303. CASH (☒ FROM) (☐ TO) BORROWER: >>		**5,154.10**	**603. CASH (☒ TO) (☐ FROM) SELLER:** >>		**39,379.24**

TAXPAYER IDENTIFICATION NUMBER SOLICITATION: SELLER

You are required by law to provide settlement agent with your correct taxpayer identification number. If you do not provide settlement agent with your correct taxpayer identification number, you may be subject to civil or criminal penalties imposed by law.
Under penalties of perjury, I certify that the number shown on this statement is my correct taxpayer identification number.

—————————————   —————————————   —————————————
Seller's Signature   Seller's Signature   Seller's Signature

The information contained in Blocks E,G,H,I and on line 401 (or if line 401 has an asterisk, line 403 and 404) is important tax information and is being furnished to the Internal Revenue Service. If you are required to file a return, a negligence penalty or other sanction will be imposed on you if this item is required to be reported and the IRS determines that it has not been reported.

Table 8.3 Settlement Charges

				PAID FROM BORROWER'S FUNDS SETTLEMENT	PAID FROM SELLER'S FUNDS SETTLEMENT
700. TOTAL SALES\BROKER'S COMMISSION:					
BASED ON PRICE $		@ %=			
DIVISION OF COMMISSION (LINE 700) AS FOLLOWS:					
701. $	to				
702. $	to				
703. Commission paid at settlement					
704.					
800. ITEMS PAYABLE IN CONNECTION WITH LOAN:			POC		
801. Loan origination fee	%			2,600.00	
802. Loan discount	%				
803. Appraisal fee to:			250.00		
804. Credit report to:					
805. Lender's inspection fee					
806. Mortgage insurance application fee to					
807. Assumption fee					
808. Commission 3% of $209700.00	to				6,291.00
809. Underwriting Fee	to			315.00	
810. Yls.Sprd.Pd. by Investaid	to		1992.15		
811. Processing Fee	to			395.00	
900. ITEMS REQUIRED BY LENDER TO BE PAID IN ADVANCE:					
901. Interest from 10/30/2002 to 11/01/2002	@ $ 47.0400 \day			94.08	
902. Mortgage insurance premium for	mos. to				
903. Hazard insurance premium for	yrs. to	Insurance	415.		
904. Flood Insurance Premium for	yrs. to				
905.					
1000. RESERVES DEPOSITED WITH LENDER:					
1001. Hazard Insurance	months @ $	per month			
1002. Mortgage insurance	months @ $	per month			
1003. City property taxes	months @ $	per month			
1004. County property taxes	months @ $	per month			
1005. Annual assessments	months @ $	per month			
1006.	months @ $	per month			
1007.	months @ $	per month			
1008.	months @ $	per month			
1100. TITLE CHARGES:					
1101. Settlement or closing fee to				300.00	
1102. Abstract or title search to					
1103. Title examination to					
1104. Title insurance binder to					
1105. Document preparation to					
1106. Notary fees to					
1107. Attorney's fees to					
(includes above items Numbers:					
1108. Title insurance to				925.00	25.00
(includes endorsements:					
1109. Lender's coverage $ 199,215.00	($925.00)				
1110. Owner's coverage $ 209,700.00	($25.00)				
1111.					
1112.					
1113.					
1200. GOVERNMENT RECORDING AND TRANSFER CHARGES:					
1201. Recording fees: Deed $12.00 : Mortgage $37.00 : Releases $				49.00	
1202. City\county tax \ stamps: Deed $ 46.20 : Mortgage $				46.20	
1203. State tax\stamps Deed $ 315.00 : Mortgage $				315.00	
1204. Recording Realease of Lien Title Company					9.00
1205.					
1300. ADDITIONAL SETTLEMENT CHARGES:					
1301. Survey to				125.00	
1302. Pest inspection to					
1303. Courier Fee to				50.00	25.00
1304. Flood Certification to				20.00	
1305.					
1306.					
1307.					
1400. TOTAL SETTLEMENT CHARGES (Enter on line 103, Section J-and-line 502, Section K) >>				5,234.28	6,350.00

I have carefully reviewed the HUD-1 Settlement Statement and to the best of my knowledge and belief, it is a true and accurate statement of all receipts and disbursements made on my account or by me in this transaction. I further certify that I have received a copy of the HUD-1 Settlement Statement.

Borrower _____ Date /0-30-02 Seller _____ Date /0/30/02

Symphony Homes Real Estate Group, L.L.C.

Borrower _____ Date 10-30-02 Seller BY: _____ Date _____
Stephen Berges

The HUD-1 Settlement Statement which I have prepared is a true and accurate account of this transaction. I have caused the funds to be disbursed in accordance with this statement. Co-Manager

Settlement Agent: _____ Date 10/30/2002

WARNING: It is a crime to knowingly make false statements to the United States on this or any other similar form. Penalties upon conviction can include a fine and imprisonment. For details see: Title 18 U.S. Code Section 1001 and Section 1010.

PAGE 2

Table 8.4 Purchaser's Statement

FILE NUMBER: SETTLEMENT DATE: 10/30/2002
CLOSER: PRORATION DATE: 10/30/2002

NAME OF PURCHASER:

NAME OF SELLER: Symphony Homes Real Estate Group, L.L.C.

NAME OF LENDER:

LOCATION OF PROPERTY: Davison, Genesee County, Michigan 48433
LAUREL HEIGHTS CONDOMINIUM as recorded in Liber 3485, Pages 942 to 1002 Genesee

	POC	AMOUNTS	TOTALS
Contract sales price......			42,000.00
Personal property......			167,700.00
PLUS CHARGES:			
Proration of City/Town taxes from 10/30/2002 to 07/01/2003		12.11	
Proration of County taxes from 10/30/2002 to 01/01/2003		5.70	
Condo Dues Pro-Rata 10/30/02-12/31/02		17.01	
Loan origination to Corporation		2,600.00	
Underwriting Fee to Corporation		315.00	
Processing Fee to Corporation		395.00	
Interest from 10/30/2002 to 11/01/2002: 2 days @ 47.0400/day		94.08	
to			
Settlement Fee to Title		300.00	
Title Insurance Premium to Company		925.00	
Lender's Coverage 199,215.00 ($925.00)			
Deed Recording Fee to Company		12.00	
Mortgage Recording Fee to Company		37.00	
City/County Deed Conveyance Tax to Genesee County Treasurer		46.20	
State Deed Conveyance Tax to Genesee County Treasurer		315.00	
Survey to Engineering Inc		125.00	
Courier Fee to Title		50.00	
Flood Certification to Corporation		20.00	
TOTAL CHARGES			5,269.10
GROSS AMOUNT DUE FROM PURCHASER...			214,969.10
LESS CREDITS:			
Deposit or earnest money		10,600.00	
Principal amount of new loan		199,215.00	
TOTAL CREDITS			209,815.00
BALANCE DUE FROM PURCHASER.......			$5,154.10

Table 8.5 Seller's Statement

FILE NUMBER:	SETTLEMENT DATE:	10/30/2002
CLOSER:	PRORATION DATE:	10/30/2002

NAME OF PURCHASER:

NAME OF SELLER: Symphony Homes Real Estate Group, L.L.C.

NAME OF LENDER:

LOCATION OF PROPERTY: Davison, Genesee County, Michigan 48433
LAUREL HEIGHTS CONDOMINIUM as recorded in Liber 3485, Pages 942 to 1002 Genesee

	POC	AMOUNTS	TOTALS
Contract sales price..			42,000.00
Personal property...			167,700.00
PLUS CREDITS:			
Proration of City/Town taxes from 10/30/2002 to 07/01/2003.................		12.11	
Proration of County taxes from 10/30/2002 to 01/01/2003....................		5.70	
Condo Dues Pro-Rata 10/30/02-12/31/02......................................		17.01	
TOTAL CREDITS.................			34.82
GROSS AMOUNT DUE TO SELLER....			209,734.82
LESS CHARGES:			
Deposit or earnest money...		10,600.00	
Payoff Ln. #1534/Acct.#211-Stock Building Supply, LLC.......................		153,316.56	
Sewer & Water Due 11/5/02...		14.02	
Sewer & Water Escrow..		75.00	
Commission 3% of $209700.00 to Company........................		6,291.00	
Title Insurance Premium to Company.....................		25.00	
Owner's Coverage 209,700.00 ($25.00)			
Recording Realease of Lien to		9.00	
Courier Fee to		25.00	
TOTAL CHARGES............................			170,355.58
BALANCE DUE TO SELLER.....................			$39,379.24

Symphony Homes Real Estate Group, L.L.C.
By: _Stephen A. Berges_   By: _____
Stephen Berges
Its: Co-Manager   Its: _____

Although I thoroughly review all of the charges on the statement, this is one in particular that I am very careful to check for accuracy.

The lender is responsible for preparing the *deed of trust* and the *promissory note*. These documents outline the terms and conditions under which the lender has agreed to loan you money. Repayment terms are specified, including the amount of the loan, the interest rate and amortization period, and any prepayment penalties that may be imposed. Other lender requirements that may also be included are escrow conditions for taxes and insurance, minimum insurance amounts, standard of care for property condition, and default provisions.

By taking the time to more fully understand all of the requisite closing documents, you will be better prepared to ensure that the closing for the investment property you are purchasing will go smoothly. For the most part, you can have confidence in the expertise of those individuals who are preparing all of the related forms, but you must also keep in mind that these individuals are human and prone to make mistakes just like anyone else. Protect your interests by carefully reviewing all of the closing documents. Doing so may potentially save you thousands of dollars.

> Set a goal to become a millionaire for what it makes of you to achieve it. Do it for the skills you have to learn and the person you have to become. Do it for what you'll end up knowing about the marketplace, what you'll learn about the management of time and working with people. Do it for the ability of discovering how to keep your ego in check. For what you have to learn about being benevolent. Being kind as well as being strong. What you have to learn about society and business and government and taxes and becoming an accomplished person to reach the status of millionaire is what's valuable. Not the million dollars.
>
> *—Earl Shoaf*

Chapter 9

Assemble a Winning Team of Professionals

$\mathbb{T}$ o truly be successful as a real estate investor, you need to assemble a winning team of professionals. If you are buying and selling only one or two properties a year, as is true for most investors, you will be involved in much of the work yourself. As you begin to participate in more and more transactions, however, you will soon discover that you can no longer do everything by yourself. In fact, you will find that the best use of your time is coordinating the efforts of others. By delegating some of the responsibilities to your team, you are able to achieve much more than if you try to do everything yourself. For example, an ox by itself can pull only a single covered wagon, but two oxen yoked together can pull several wagons. This well-established principle can be summarized as, "The sum of the parts is greater than the whole." It is a phenomenon known as *synergy*. Synergistic effects are created when individuals who might otherwise work independently instead work together. The individuals are able to achieve much more working together in a collective effort than they can on their own. (See Exhibit 9.1.)

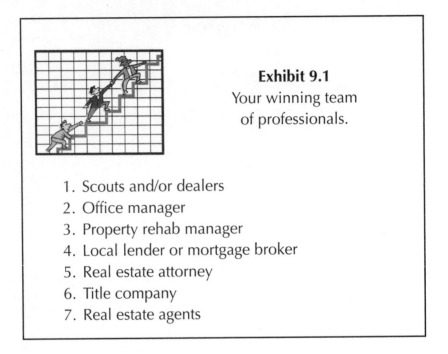

Exhibit 9.1
Your winning team
of professionals.

1. Scouts and/or dealers
2. Office manager
3. Property rehab manager
4. Local lender or mortgage broker
5. Real estate attorney
6. Title company
7. Real estate agents

SCOUTS AND/OR DEALERS

Perhaps the most important element of your winning team of professionals is to have dedicated scouts and dealers working in your behalf. You may recall from Chapter 2 that both scouts and dealers can provide you with a steady source of property leads. Leads from these sources and others are the lifeblood of your business. Without them, it will be very difficult to be successful in the business of flipping properties. You should work to build relationships with several different scouts and dealers. You also need to take time to establish investment criteria that best suits your objectives so that the individuals you are working with know what types of opportunities to present to you. You don't want them spending needless time on deals that you have no interest in. Furthermore, you don't want to waste your time by looking at deals that don't meet your needs.

The relationship between you and other scouts and dealers is mutually beneficial. The more opportunities they bring you, the more you will buy from them or from those they recommend, and the more you buy from them, the more money they will make. It is a win-win relationship. You may also decide to hire a full-time scout of your own. In addition to paying a small base wage, I recommend implementing an incentive system in which your scout is rewarded for every deal he or she brings you that you end up buying. Your scout will quickly learn exactly what kind of opportunities you are most interested in and bring you only the cream of the crop.

OFFICE MANAGER

An effective office manager is another key individual on your winning team of professionals. Before you can have a good office manager, though, you first have to have an office. Most people who invest in real estate start out buying and selling a little at a time. As their capital base grows, so does their ability to increase the volume of transactions. At some point in the process, it will become necessary to discontinue your part-time operation out of your home office and begin a full-time operation out of an office building. When you reach that point in your business, I recommend that one of the first people you hire is an office manager. You can delegate many of the lesser responsibilities to him or her, which in turn enables you to focus on growing your business. Office managers can handle many of the more repetitive day-to-day tasks that can take up so much of your time. They can furthermore be trained over time to take on greater responsibilities, such as some of the accounting and marketing functions.

A good office manager can also be trained to perform functions like scheduling and coordinating all of the necessary parties involved in a closing, as well as attending the closings for you. You may initially be uncomfortable turning that responsibility over to another person, but after your fiftieth or so closing, chances are you'll be more receptive to the idea of having someone attend them for you. I find that while most closings go smoothly, they typically require a minimum of no less than two hours of my time. By the time I drive to the title company, wait for the closing officer to finish preparing the documents, sign off on everything, and drive back to my office, I have at least two hours invested in the process, and sometimes more. While selling and closing the deal excites me, I find sitting around in title companies to be quite boring. Hire a good office manager and use your time where it counts the most, buying and selling properties.

PROPERTY REHAB MANAGER

I cannot stress enough the importance of hiring a rehab manager. This person will "take the rehab out of rehabbing" for you. The property rehab manager's primary role is to coordinate and schedule the subcontractors for all of the required renovations. A handyman is often the most well-qualified person for this type of job. You want somebody managing the crews who can determine what exactly needs to be done, and then to make sure that the repairs are done correctly. A handyman can also save you money by doing a lot of the smaller repairs personally; however, this depends on the number of houses you have undergoing repairs at any given time. If you have several houses being worked on simultaneously, a rehab manager may not have time to do any of the repairs. On the other hand, if you only have two or three in progress at any given time, then your rehab manager will most likely be able to make some of the repairs while at the same time scheduling the other contractors. Remember that the most effective use of your time is not to fix the houses yourself, but rather to oversee the efforts of those who do. By hiring a property rehab manager, you are in effect delegating that responsibility to someone else. This allows you to focus on building your business.

LOCAL LENDER OR MORTGAGE BROKER

Another very important component of your real estate business is financing. For this reason, it is essential for you to have one or more lenders or mortgage brokers as members of your winning team of professionals. You must have access to capital—and preferably to large sources of it. It usually becomes necessary to establish relationships with several lenders or mortgage brokers to meet your growing needs for financing. In the initial stages of your relationship, you will most likely secure financing on a case-by-case basis. As the lender becomes more comfortable with you, however, the process of obtaining financing becomes much easier.

Unless you already have a strong personal balance sheet, these types of relationships are not formed overnight. They can sometimes take years to form. I am very fortunate in that I currently have the ability to pick up the phone and secure financing within about five minutes for many of the projects I am involved in. Access to capital is vital to your success in this business. Work hard to establish sound relationships with lenders in your area who can provide you with the financing needed to enable you to be successful.

REAL ESTATE ATTORNEY

Another member of your winning team of professionals that you will want to consider is a real estate attorney. The yellow pages are full of attorneys, most of whom advertise the area of law they specialize in. Look for one who specifically advertises real estate services. A few minutes on the phone will give you an idea of an attorney's level of expertise. Don't be intimidated just because someone carries the title of attorney. It is quite likely that you know as much about real estate in general as any given attorney. You hope, of course, that the one you choose is more knowledge-able about real estate law. I prefer to work with attorneys who own investment property themselves. This gives them an added level of experience. Adding this individual to your team of professionals will provide you with the legal expertise needed from time to time during the course of your business.

TITLE COMPANY

A competent title company is another essential member of your winning team of professionals. While most title companies offer similar services (providing title insurance and closing services, etc.), they vary greatly on the degree to which they can provide those services. Over the years, I have worked with many different title companies. Each one seems to have its own unique set of nuances.

Until recently, I had a relationship with a national title company that had a deplorable operations department. The firm's outside salesman contacted me and wooed me over to this company. The salesman, Derek, was himself a shining example of what it means to be customer focused. He was extremely attentive to me individually and was proficient in addressing all of my needs and concerns. "This is great," I thought. "Here's a guy who really cares about his customers and is always willing to go the extra mile for them." What I didn't know, however, was that while Derek was about as good an outside salesman you could hope for, the company's operations department was just the opposite. I sent them seven or eight deals right off the bat and ended up having problems with almost every one of them. I had problems with scheduled closings that had been confirmed for a certain date and then mysteriously disappeared from the company's book. I had problems with the people in operations who were supposed to be capable of preparing all the title work, but just couldn't seem to get it right. And finally, I had problems with incapable closing officers. Derek was great. The rest of the company was a mess.

Now that I've lamented my poor experience with this particular (unnamed) company, let me conclude on a more positive note. The title company that I have since switched to is quite the opposite. For the most part, I can send this company a deal, schedule it, and show up at the closing with everything properly prepared and in order. Although I pay a little more for the title services of this company, it's worth it to me. I don't have nearly the headaches and frustrations that I did with the previous company. Find a competent title company in your area and include it on your winning team of professionals.

REAL ESTATE AGENTS

Top-producing real estate agents are vital elements of your winning team of professionals. You should plan to include as many of them as possible on your team. If an agent knows you are a serious buyer, he or she will work to bring you the types of deals you are most interested in. As with scouts and dealers, you must establish predetermined criteria that meet your investment objectives. The better your sales agents understand exactly what you are looking for, the better they will be able to meet your investment needs.

If you limit yourself to just one agent, then you have only one set of eyes and ears on the lookout for good deals to bring to you. On the other hand, if you enlist the aid of several real estate agents, you will increase the number of potential investment opportunities that you can take advantage of. Each agent has his or her own sphere of influence—friends and associates with whom they interact on a daily basis. You never know when one of them will come across that gem of a deal just waiting to be discovered.

When it becomes time for you to sell your property, you will also likely want to have more than one agent working in your behalf. Those of you who are licensed agents are likely to disagree with me on this point, but please allow me to explain. The reason I prefer to use more than one agent is because I know that agents tend to specialize in certain areas by farming specific communities. Yes, I know, you can list the property for sale in the MLS just like any other agent and gain access to a broad spectrum of buyers, which is certainly very important, but unless you are familiar with the area in which you have the listing and physically work that area, you are doing your seller a disservice.

I have seen, for example, agents take listings clear across the county and even into the neighboring counties. These areas may be as far as 50 miles from where they live and work. No matter how hard you try, you can't convince me that you can effectively sell a house for me in an area about which you know little or nothing. Your marketing efforts will be limited to a few newspaper ads and to the MLS. Agents selling in faraway markets are likely to have no personal contacts or relationships in that area. They know absolutely nothing about the town or city except the name of it. They know nothing about the school district, which is vital information to anyone with children. Chances are, they haven't even been to the community except to write the listing agreement. Yet I see this all the time—a real estate sign placed in a homeowner's yard by someone I know good and well is not from that area. To be successful in the business of buying and selling investment properties, it is essential for you to include several real estate agents who can create a pipeline of inventory for you, as well as represent you effectively when it becomes time to sell.

In summary, we have examined the merits of building a first-class team of people who can help mobilize you to effectively reach your investment objectives. Each member of the team is vital for your success in the real estate business. You may initially go through a trial-and-error period in which some members of the team have to be replaced for one reason or another. In time, however, you will eventually assemble a winning team of professionals who when working together can help you achieve much more than you could ever hope to on your own.

> Few people are capable of expressing with equanimity opinions which differ from the prejudices of their social environment. Most people are even incapable of forming such opinions.
>
> —*Albert Einstein*

Chapter 10

Three Keys to Maximizing Your Potential

There are three important keys that when properly applied will empower you to maximize your potential as it relates to buying and selling houses. In this chapter, I examine several postentry strategies that you should seriously consider long before you close on the property. I also analyze the advantages and disadvantages of doing the required repairs yourself versus hiring others to do it. Finally, I review several methods to increase the marketability of your property. The proper and systematic application of the three precepts outlined in this chapter will enable you to maximize your potential in the real estate arena. (See Exhibit 10.1.)

POSTENTRY PLANNING

Your postentry strategy is the specific plan of action you will take immediately after the closing of your property. I want to emphasize the word *immediately*. Remember that time is of the essence and every day that passes by without being fully used costs you money. This is why you must plan well in advance of the closing date for the work required to prepare the property for its eventual

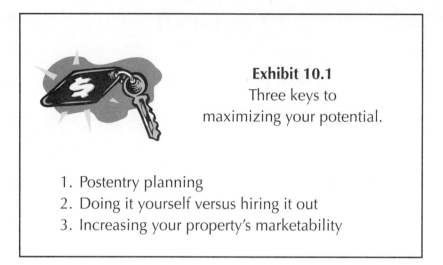

Exhibit 10.1
Three keys to
maximizing your potential.

1. Postentry planning
2. Doing it yourself versus hiring it out
3. Increasing your property's marketability

resale. Minimizing the turnaround time on each deal is crucial to helping you maximize your profits.

One of the best ways to begin preparing is by scheduling the contractors who will be making the repairs (assuming you are not doing the work yourself) two to three weeks before the scheduled closing date if possible. Don't make the mistake of waiting until after you close to begin thinking about scheduling. You will lose valuable time by doing so, and remember, time is money because you are paying interest on the borrowed funds. The best time to tentatively begin the scheduling process is when the contractors first come out to the property to provide you with bids for the work to be performed. This data, as you recall, is used in your assessment of the viability of the project. After factoring in all the costs and expenses related to the project, as well as market comparables, then and only then are you able to accurately measure the expected return in profits that a particular project will generate.

When you meet with the contractors, you can provide them at that time with a general idea of when you expect to close. Be sure to express to the contractors how important it is for them to be available when you need them. Explain to them that you prefer not to lose even a single day. Once you have established a firm closing date with the seller and the title company, you can then schedule a specific date and time for your contractor to make the repairs. The key is to establish your postentry plan well in advance and to be prepared to execute it as soon after the closing as possible.

DOING IT YOURSELF VERSUS HIRING IT OUT

Is it better to do the work yourself and try to save money or to hire as much of the work out as possible and try to save time? This is a question that many real estate investors struggle with, especially those who are just starting out. While there is no single right answer, it's important to understand the advantages and disadvantages of both methods.

For those of you who may be more mechanically inclined, it is natural for you to feel and believe that you should do much of the work yourself in an effort to save money. Allow me to share a personal example with you of the differences between two individuals who have different skill sets. The first individual is my brother, Tim, who has very strong mechanical skills and can fix almost anything. In fact, one of my earliest memories of him "fixing" something occurred when I was about three years old. Tim would have been five at the time. I remember coming outside to play one day only to discover that he had taken all the wheels off my shiny red tricycle. Another time, he completely disassembled our swing set. While Tim was exceptionally good at taking things apart, he had unfortunately not yet learned how to put them back together, thereby rendering my tricycle and the swing set useless. Tim has come a long way since that time. Not only has he become an expert at taking things apart, but he is now extremely proficient at putting them back together.

The second individual in this example is none other than yours truly. While I lack the natural mechanical skills that Tim has, I do have very good organizational and management skills. I recall that in my teenage years I was always very particular about keeping my bedroom as neat and orderly as possible. I was probably the only child in the family who made my bed without having to be asked to do so. My personality demanded structure and order. Later, my service in the U.S. Air Force reinforced these concepts, especially the training I received at boot camp (also known as basic training) at Lackland Air Force Base in San Antonio, Texas. Our beds had to be made perfectly with blankets folded taut enough to literally bounce a quarter off of. Everything in our foot-lockers had to be placed in exact and precise order according to our training manuals. If it wasn't, believe me, you would hear about it from the drill sergeant.

I never will forget one experience in my early days in basic training. I had only been there a few days and had just received my air force fatigues, which were all green. Since they were brand new, none of the insignia had been sewn on yet. With our heads freshly shaven and our new uniforms not yet adorned with insignia, we were referred to as "pickles," because that is exactly what we looked like, a bunch of green dill pickles running around. Anyway, being brand new in the service, I was not fully aware of all the rules. My drill sergeant's name was Sergeant Carter, and believe it or not, he bore a strong resemblance in both manner and appearance to the Sergeant Carter in the old TV sitcom, *Gomer Pyle.* One afternoon while wearing my fatigues, I put a pencil in my shirt pocket. After all, that's what pockets are for, right? Wrong! Little did I know that I was out of uniform. That's right, that little pencil sticking out of my pocket was not supposed to be there, and boy, did Sergeant Carter let me know about it. He literally stood nose to nose with me and bellowed out something like, "Airman, what's wrong with you!?! Don't you know you're out of uniform! You better get that #*!#*!#*! pencil out of your #*!#*!#* pocket and don't ever let me see it in there again! Do you understand me?" "Yes, sir!" came my immediate reply, and believe me, he never did see that pencil in my pocket again because I wasn't about to put it in there and run the risk of another verbal thrashing. In fact, to this very day, I sometimes have second thoughts about putting a pencil in my shirt pocket.

With Tim's strong mechanical skills, he has quite naturally developed a mind-set to fix or repair things himself, including his rental properties. After all, why pay somebody to come in and rehab a house when you can do it yourself and save money? I must say that I have to give him credit for taking on some tough jobs. Over the years, I've observed Tim take on bathroom and kitchen remodeling, replace badly worn flooring, do tiling, and perform painting, roofing, plumbing, and air-conditioning work. I'm sure I've left some things out of that list, but you can name just about anything having to do with repairing a house and Tim has done it.

On the other hand, I have done a few things such as painting and mowing the lawn, but I don't hesitate to call in the pros to take on the other work. First, I don't have the skills necessary to perform some of the more involved repairs. Second, I don't have the desire to do them. This is not to say that I couldn't learn how to make some of the more complex repairs, but I have no desire to. As one who is naturally well organized and possesses good management skills, I much prefer to call in the proper tradesperson and pay him or her to do the work. I consider this to be a much better use of my time than trying to do the work myself. Because I naturally enjoy planning and preparing for upcoming events, I take the time (long before I close on a property) to ensure that my tradespeople, who are all more skilled than I am when it comes to fixing houses, are ready to perform the work as soon as I need them. For me, this is a much more efficient process than trying to do everything myself.

I recall one time in particular when Tim had just purchased a single-family house that he was going to renovate and subsequently flip. About the same time, I had just purchased an apartment building that was also in need of some extensive rehab work. Tim, Mr. Do-It-Yourself, was committed to doing most of the rehab work by himself. Although he did have a little bit of help, Tim did most of the work on his own. I, on the other hand,

Mr. Hire-Everything-Out, was committed to doing none of the work myself and hiring all of it out. Since Tim had a full-time job, he was able to work on the house only after work and on weekends. As I recall, he gave up nights and weekends for three or four months to make the necessary renovations and prepare the house for resale. Meanwhile, I had all of the bids in for the required repairs on my apartment building before I had even closed, and I was ready to go the day after closing. Within about 30 to 45 days, the tradespeople were completely finished with the repair work and my property was ready for resale. In addition, since the building was fully occupied by tenants, I began initiating increases in the rents, which were justified by the recently completed improvements.

This example is meant to be an observation of fact only and is certainly not intended as a criticism of my brother, Tim, whom I love dearly. It is instead intended to illustrate the differences in the way the same tasks can be accomplished. Tim has his way of doing things, and I have my way of doing things. While Tim is saving money, I am saving time. To me, time is money, so I am really saving both time and money. To flip properties on a large scale, you cannot possibly do all of the required repairs yourself. You must decide if you are in the business of fixing houses or of buying and selling houses. If it is the latter, then you cannot afford to spend your time doing the repairs. The only exception to this may be when you are first getting started and are only doing one or two houses a year. At that level, you can probably justify taking the time to do some of the work on your own, but once you start ramping up your operation, you must begin scaling back your hands-on involvement and take care to make the best and most valuable use of your time, which is to organize and manage. Once you have your tradespeople in place and have fine-tuned your system, you have the ability to do 10, 20, 50, or even 100 houses per year.

Although it may initially appear that an investor would be giving up some of the profits by hiring out the rehab work, this is not necessarily the case. The key is to purchase the property at the right price to begin with. In Chapter 6, I provided several examples of appropriate analysis methods to be used when selecting an investment property. I recommend that you factor into your analysis of potential investment opportunities the cost of having contractors do the required repairs. If your analysis does not provide an acceptable rate of return on your invested capital, then you simply pass on it and move on to the next deal. Do *not* fall into the trap of rationalizing your analysis by saying that since you really like this deal, you will go ahead and do all of the painting, for example, just to make the numbers work out. You are much better off passing on it and waiting for another opportunity, for it will surely come.

INCREASING YOUR PROPERTY'S MARKETABILITY

Congratulations! You've worked hard over the past few weeks or months renovating your investment property. You have increased the house's value by a significant amount, and it is now time to sell it and capture the profit margin that you have created! You can do several things to enhance the marketability of your property and to increase the exposure it receives. These include preplanning, heightened visibility through the MLS, offering a marketable product, pricing your property competitively, and offering incentives. (See Exhibit 10.2.)

Preplanning

Proper planning from start to finish is essential for you to be successful in this business. This includes planning for the sale of your property. After all, you are not rewarded for your efforts until the sale has been completed. Only then do you profit from your labors. You may be thinking that of course you are going to plan to sell your house, but you'd be surprised at how many investors wait until they get to that phase of the process before

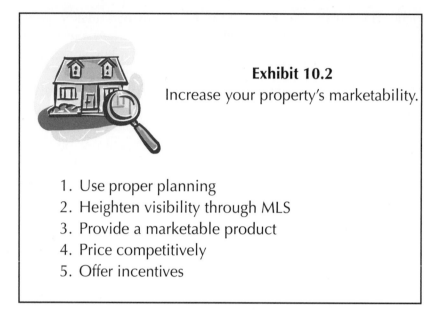

Exhibit 10.2
Increase your property's marketability.

1. Use proper planning
2. Heighten visibility through MLS
3. Provide a marketable product
4. Price competitively
5. Offer incentives

they even begin to consider how they will sell their property. Earlier in this chapter ("Postentry Planning"), I discussed the necessity of scheduling your subcontractors long before the actual closing occurred so that you would be ready to go with your improvements immediately following the consummation of the sale. Planning your exit strategy is equally important, if not more so, than the postentry strategy. Ideally, you should begin thinking about how you are going to sell your house even before you purchase it. You should already have taken the steps to establish a well-defined sales plan so that you are ready to implement it immediately at the appropriate time.

Heightening Visibility through the MLS

The Multiple Listing Service (MLS) is a requisite tool to provide your property with maximum exposure. This means, of course, that you will have to list your property for sale with a licensed real estate agent, unless you happen to be a licensed agent yourself. When your house is placed in the MLS, you gain immediate access to hundreds and even thousands of sales agents who have a potential interest in your property. Any one of them may have a prospective buyer with whom they are working who may be interested in exactly what you are selling. You cannot afford to forgo having your house listed for sale in the MLS. Remember that you are in the business of buying houses, refurbishing them, and selling them as quickly as possible. Your role in this business should be that of a manager. You are there to facilitate the process and to ensure that things happen when they are supposed to happen. You can certainly make the argument that you can save money by not having to pay the sales agent's commission, but that would be a weak argument at best. Using that logic, you are reverting to the "I can do it myself and save money" mode. Trying to sell the house yourself and save money is no different than trying to do all of the repairs yourself and save money. That rationale is shortsighted and will prevent you from maximizing your potential in this business. If you are not a licensed real estate agent already, I recommend you find a top-producing agent who has a proven track record of being a mover and a shaker. In other words, look for a competent agent who is serious about helping you sell your properties as quickly as possible. In Chapter 2, I described the role of the dealer as it relates to flipping properties. I mentioned that while dealers can be a good source for bringing you investment opportunities, they can also be a good source for selling those properties for you once the necessary improvements have been made. Dealers are particularly fond of this type of relationship as it enables them to double-dip, meaning that not only do they earn a commission when they sell the property *to* you, but they also earn a commission when they sell the property *for* you. If you have a good relationship with sales agents or dealers and are listing several properties with them on a continuing basis, chances are they will be willing to negotiate their fee structure with you. The most important thing for you here is to maximize the visibility of the property you are selling so that you can gain ready access to as large a pool of buyers as possible.

Offering a Marketable Product

To further enhance the marketability of your house, you must offer a product that people want. As simple as this may sound, this is an important point that shouldn't be taken lightly. Recall from Chapter 3 that as an investor who is in the business of flipping properties, you are not interested in carrying your inventory any longer than necessary. That means you should carefully study the area in which you are considering investing to determine which vicinities are selling with the shortest average number of days on the market. The type of location best suited for selling your properties in a timely manner is typically a neighborhood between 10 and 30 years old. These neighborhoods are where the average middle-class citizen lives. The ideal location is one in which the majority of homes are well maintained and that is is not suffering from functional obsolescence. The area should be well established, have good schools nearby, and continue to have homes that sell on average in fewer days than those of surrounding communities. Characteristics of this kind of neighborhood often include mature landscaping, pristine lawns, and well-cared-for homes. Be sure that the house you purchase fits in with the rest of the houses in the neighborhood. I have seen, for example, an ultracontemporary house in a mostly traditional neighborhood sit on the market much longer than other houses in the same neighborhood. You can't wait, of course, to make these kinds of decisions when it's time to sell. They must be made long before you even buy. In addition, your investment property should be presented to prospective buyers in its most favorable condition. Common sense dictates that after all of the subcontractors have finished their work, you must be willing to spend a little extra on a good cleaning service to put the finishing touches on your house to make it really look like new. Housecleaning services typically do not cost much, and it is money well spent.

Competitive Pricing

If you did your homework before purchasing your investment property, you should already be intimately familiar with pricing in your market. I recommend making your house available for sale at a price just below market. As an investor who is in the business of flipping properties, you do not have time to sit on your house for an indefinite period in an attempt to hold out for top dollar. Remember that you have carrying costs, including interest, taxes, and insurance, so the quicker you sell the quicker you can relieve yourself of those obligations. In addition, you have an *opportunity cost,* meaning that as long as your investment capital is tied up in one property, you are limited in your ability to take advantage of other opportunities. You have become capitally constrained. Time is money in this business, so the quicker you can sell your property, the more money you will be capable of making.

Offering Incentives

If you are like most people, chances are you are motivated by money. Your prospective buyers will be motivated by money, too. You can use many different types of incentives that have some monetary value to encourage prospective buyers to purchase your house instead of the one down the street. For example, you can offer a credit at closing for landscaping. This will enable the buyers to beautify the exterior of their new home shortly after they move in. For many buyers, especially those who are first-time home buyers, it takes everything they have financially just to move in, so they will greatly appreciate having a little extra at closing. Whether the money is used for landscaping or any other purpose is really irrelevant. Your objective is to give them a reason to buy your house now rather than continuing to shop around. Other incentives include agreeing to pay the buyer's closing costs (or a portion of them), offering to throw in free appliances, or giving them a gift certificate from a local moving company to help offset their moving expenses.

SUMMARY

In summary, we have discussed the three most important keys that, when properly applied, will enable you to maximize your potential in the real estate business. We examined a variety of postentry strategies, analyzed the advantages and disadvantages of doing the necessary repairs yourself versus hiring the work out, and reviewed several methods to increase the marketability of your property. The three principles outlined in this chapter will enable you to maximize your potential in the real estate arena when regularly and consistently applied. Each of these essential elements takes time to master. You must be willing not only to apply yourself, but to be patient as you do so. Life is full of adversities and challenges that can test the measure of who we are. We must be willing to meet these challenges with courage and determination. We must be prepared to respond, not to react, to adverse circumstances. When we rise up to meet whatever challenges life presents us with, then and only then do we become victorious. Then and only then are our characters and our moral fiber strengthened. Then and only then can we become the kind of people that we truly wish to become.

> I hope that I shall always possess firmness and virtue enough to maintain what I consider the most enviable of all titles, the character of an honest man.
> —*George Washington*

Chapter 11

The Three Principles of Power

In Chapter 10 of my previous book, *The Complete Guide to Buying and Selling Apartment Buildings*, I wrote about the five keys to your success as follows:

> The central focus of this book is on arming you with the specific tools necessary to identify potential acquisition candidates, to acquire and manage those properties once identified, to implement sound techniques for creating value, and finally, to capture all of that value, or as much of it as possible, through various exit strategies. The process by which all of this can be accomplished rests, I believe, on five keys that are crucial to success. These keys do not deal with the mechanical processes involved in buying and selling apartment buildings, but are grounded in principles fundamental to life itself. These laws deal with the human psyche. They govern our thoughts, which in turn, direct our actions. The failure to understand these keys—which can provide the foundation of happiness, and ultimately of success—will almost certainly guarantee your defeat.

The Five Keys to Success

1. Understanding risk
2. Overcoming fear of failure
3. Accepting responsibility
4. Willingness to persevere
5. Defining your sense of purpose

Although the book was comprehensive in dealing with the subject of apartment buildings, I received more correspondence from individuals who were moved and inspired by this chapter than by any other material in the book, a factor that I believe has largely contributed to its success. One such reader, David S. of West Hollywood, California, writes, "Your book has truly taught me about investing in apartment buildings, but more importantly it has taught me about life. . . . The words not only inspired this reader, but allowed me to see the importance of having a purpose." This chapter is much like Chapter 10 in *The Complete Guide to Buying and Selling Apartment Buildings.* In this chapter, I discuss what I refer to as the three principles of power. (See Figure 11.1.) These three principles have absolutely nothing to do with real estate in particular, yet everything to do with your success in it. For that matter, the three principles of power can be applied to any business or profession and are not just limited to real estate. Furthermore, these laws can be used in your personal life and, when properly applied, can be a source of great joy and happiness to you and to those with whom you associate.

Although I have a passion for investing in real estate, the things that I write in this chapter are far more important to me than finding the next house to buy or sell. These principles lie at the very core of my belief system. They are an integral part of who I am. They compel me each and every day to strive for a perfection that I know I will never achieve in this life. It is my hope to inspire you to incorporate these three principles of power into your belief system. Doing so will enable you to reach the highest level of achievement of which you are truly capable. You will be empow-

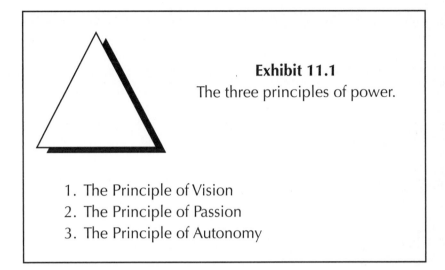

Exhibit 11.1
The three principles of power.

1. The Principle of Vision
2. The Principle of Passion
3. The Principle of Autonomy

ered to fulfill the measure of your creation, to reach your potential, and to enjoy the abundant gifts life has to offer.

The three principles of power can best be illustrated by sharing with you an example of how one man I knew applied them in his life. The principle of vision, the principle of passion, and the principle of autonomy are all embodied within his story. Although this individual is relatively unknown in corporate America's public business circles, he has had a profound impact on the retailing industry. He is, in fact, directly responsible for creating the largest and most successful single retail store in America! You may be thinking of Sam Walton, the founder of Wal-Mart. This is not Sam's story, however. It is instead the story of Jim "Mattress Mack" McIngvale. "Who is he?" you ask. If you've lived in or visited Houston, Texas, in the past 20 to 25 years, chances are you know who Mattress Mack is. His 30-second commercials on radio and television air continuously, averaging one every seven minutes of every hour, or about 200 a day! Jim McIngvale is the creator and founder of Houston-based Gallery Furniture. With annual sales in excess of $200 million, his single-site furniture store sells more furniture per square foot of retail space than any other store in the world!

I lived in Houston for a number of years and was thus exposed to at least a portion of Gallery's 200-plus commercials a day. I had always been impressed with the remarkable success of Jim McIngvale. Although I didn't know Jim personally, his face became a familiar sight, as he did all of his own commercials, which were always the low-budget type, with no paid actors. They featured Jim jumping up and down with a wad of money in his hand and shouting, "Gallery Furniture really will save . . . you . . . money!!" Jim is also a well-known community activist and participates in and supports many events in the Houston area. For example, Jim and Gallery Furniture are official sponsors of the Houston Rockets, and they are known for purchasing the grand champion steer each year at the Houston Livestock and Rodeo Show.

It wasn't until McIngvale's *Always Think Big* was published (Dearborn Trade, 2002) that I was able to learn more about what made Mattress Mack so successful. *Always Think Big* is the story of Jim's life experiences as they relate to his business and includes the factors that contributed to his extraordinary accomplishments. The three principles of power—vision, passion, and autonomy—are exemplified in his story. Jim McIngvale, who personifies these three principles, outlines his vision for what he intends to be the largest and most successful furniture store in Houston, which he vigorously and passionately carries out through a series of independent-minded and autonomous decisions, acting against the advice of other professionals.

THE PRINCIPLE OF VISION

The principle of vision is a fundamental and essential component of the three principles of power, as it provides the very foundation that enables you to enjoy and exercise the other two precepts— passion and autonomy. The principle of vision is a priceless treasure for which there is no substitute because it enables us to see where we are going long before we get there. Vision is the tool that gives us the power to create our own destiny.

Jim McIngvale's story of building the world's most productive retail furniture store began with a vision. At the age of about 22, Jim, who had played football in high school and college, yearned to be like his father, "independent and self-reliant." In *Always Think Big,* Jim's vision of the person he wanted to become and what he wanted to do with his life had already begun. He states, "The 30-year plan of going to work for someone else was never a consideration for me. I'm an entrepreneur. I knew that I was going to start and run my own business."

Before going into the furniture business, however, Jim had suffered a devastating setback in the health club industry. His love of sports coupled with his entrepreneurial spirit led him to open six health clubs in Dallas, Texas, within a five-year period. Jim recalls, "Sometime after opening my third club, I realized I wasn't paying attention to my customers, couldn't watch or examine the business details, and failed to make many scheduled meetings." It wasn't long after that the cash flow from the health clubs began to dry up, and Jim knew that the stores were in trouble. He writes, "Finally, when the cash could no longer be shuffled from club to club, and from club to creditors at a satisfactory rate, I had to file for bankruptcy protection. I was devastated." To make matters even worse, Jim was served with divorce papers by his wife's attorney shortly thereafter. The financial stress and pressure had not only ruined him financially, but it had also ruined his family.

Jim McIngvale sold his car, broke the lease on his luxury apartment, and moved back in with his parents, stripped not only of all his worldly possessions, but also of his pride and self-esteem. He began to sink into a dark state of despair and depression. He had lost all hope and sense of purpose. His life became meaningless. In his despondent state, Jim's battered spirit suffered greater and greater emotional trauma with each passing day. His love of life, his dreams of success, his hope for a brighter future were all but lost. In *Always Think Big,* Jim writes,

I spent days at a time without leaving my parent's house. I felt like a failure. When I looked in the mirror, I thought to myself that I even looked like a failure. A mostly shy and private person already, I was now becoming even more withdrawn. Talking became a burden. My depression began to feed on itself. The more depressed I got, the less functional I became. The less functional I became, the more depressed I got. It became a vicious cycle that anyone who has suffered from depression knows all too well. I had always had something to lift my spirits when things weren't going well—football, weight lifting, business. Now I wasn't sure what to do.

After several months of moping around his parent's house, Jim's dad had finally had enough. Although he had tried to be understanding of what Jim was going through, he decided that in order for Jim to climb out of the hole of self-pity, he was going to need a good kick in the pants. Actually, what he gave Jim was a kick right out of the front door. That's right. Just like a mother bird, Jim's dad pushed him right out of the nest to force him to fly—or in this case, to get back on his feet. He gave him exactly one week to find a place and get out.

The nudge Jim's father gave him turned out to be just what he needed. With very little money, Jim decided to approach his sister, who was married and had a family to care for, about staying with her for a few days until he could figure out what he wanted to do with his life. The following Sunday morning while watching TV, Oral Roberts happened to come on. Although Jim didn't much care for television evangelism, something was different on this day. It seemed as though Oral Roberts was speaking directly to him:

Are you feeling as if you don't have the power to change? Do you feel as though you've lost control of your life? What should you do about it? Many people feel this way. The problem is, most people think small, and small results are what they get. The solution is to always think big. Think big and believe good things will happen. Think big and strive to achieve greater things each day. You have the choice. Think small and keep on getting small results, or think big and strive for goals that stretch your limits.

Oral Roberts's message was exactly what Jim needed to hear at that moment in his life. Jim had always been in the habit of thinking big and having vision, as he had with his health clubs. He had just suffered a minor and temporary setback. That was all. It was now time to get back on track. By the following Tuesday morning, he had already made up his mind about what he wanted to do. From the time he was a small boy, Jim had always been fascinated with furniture. He wasn't sure where that fascination stemmed from, but thought it probably had something to do with his mother. She constantly rearranged the furniture in the house, and from time to time, she bought new and unusual pieces with which to decorate. Jim determined right away that if he was going to open his own furniture store, he would first need to learn something about the business. He got a job at one of the local furniture stores in Dallas as a salesman and began to immediately apply himself to studying and learning everything he could about the business. After only five months, Jim McIngvale became the top sales producer in the store and was already planning his next move, which was to open his own store.

Jim had firmly believed in the message Oral Roberts delivered on that dark and lonely Sunday morning, the message of thinking big. Jim had a plan. He had a vision of opening the most successful furniture store in the city. The only problem was, he wasn't sure which city. He didn't want to compete against his former employer, who had given him an opportunity to prove himself. To fulfill his dream of owning the most successful furniture store in the city, that meant that it would have to be a different city. Jim had heard that Houston was experiencing strong growth, so he decided that's where he would have the best chance of becoming furniture king.

One of my all-time favorite quotes is by Zig Ziglar. He says, "Go as far as you can see, and when you get there, you can always see farther." Think about Zig's statement for a moment. While it is simplistic in structure, it is profound in meaning. Imagine traveling on a ship across the ocean and looking out across the vast expanse of water to the point where the sky meets the ocean. It is referred to as the *horizon*. In this case, if you "go as far as you can see," you will travel on the ship to the point where you first saw the horizon. As you travel closer to that specific point, however, you realize that the horizon is now at a point beyond where you first saw it; hence, "when you get there, you can always see farther."

Zig Ziglar's quote aptly applies to having a vision of what you want to become or of how large you want to grow your real estate business. You will naturally not have all of the answers when you first start out. Your vision begins as a tiny seed. As you water and nourish it, it will begin to grow. Just like the seed, your vision needs food and nourishment. This means that in addition to being a dreamer or a visionary, you must also be a doer. You must act on your vision or it will never bear fruit. The more you act on achieving your dreams, the clearer they will become to you. As you take steps toward fulfilling your vision, the vision will begin to crystallize and become more well defined with each passing day. "Go as far as you can see, and when you get there, you can always see farther."

That is exactly what Jim McIngvale did. He had a vision of owning and operating the largest and most successful furniture store in Houston. When Jim first started out, he didn't have all the answers. His vision was but a tiny seed. It was through his continued efforts to nourish the seed that he was able to successfully achieve his dream. With each passing day, Jim's dream became more and more vivid. It was beginning to take shape. The steps he needed to take to solidify and fulfill his dream were becoming crystal clear. Jim's approach was to do absolutely everything he could to delight the customer. His customers told him again and again that they didn't like having to wait four to six weeks for their furniture to be delivered, as was typical at other furniture stores. In *Always Think Big*, Jim describes this important aspect of his vision:

> The trickle of customers started to pick up over time, and I learned immediately that delivering furniture when the customer wants it had to become a Gallery promise. I wanted Gallery to be totally committed to same day

delivery. This was an important anchor in my plan and vision of how to succeed in the furniture business.

As Jim listened intently each and every day to what his customers were telling him, he became absolutely convinced that the same-day approach to delivering furniture was the key to his success. Not only did Jim listen to his customers for information that would help fuel the growth of his business, he also observed other successful businesses to learn what steps they had taken to achieve success. Regarding Southwest Airlines, Jim notes,

> I had observed carefully and occasionally firsthand one particular segment of Southwest Airlines' approach to customers and how they repeatedly turned around and cleaned planes to meet schedules. I believed that Southwest's approach to meeting schedules could be applied to the furniture business. Even today, the practice of most furniture stores is to take a customer's order and deliver it in about six, ten, or fifteen weeks. I knew that this gap between purchase and delivery was disappointing and frustrating to customers. Southwest Airlines cut out all the frills and provided passengers with better, faster, and cheaper service. Why not better, faster, and cheaper delivery of furniture?

That is exactly what Jim "Mattress Mack" McIngvale did. He had a vision of becoming the most successful store in Houston. He didn't start out with all of the answers, but by going as far as he could see, he was always able to go farther when he got there. Jim watered and nourished his vision by acting on the feedback his customers were giving him and by observing other successful business. Jim's vision is no longer a dream. It has become a reality. By acting on his intense vision, Gallery Furniture of Houston now delivers furniture "better, faster, and cheaper" than any other furniture store in the world. The first principle of power, the principle of vision, enabled Jim McIngvale to achieve remarkable heights in the furniture business. This principle can no doubt empower you to achieve extraordinary success in the real estate business as well. To those who would dare to dream, and dream big, Jim offers this wise counsel:

> Dreams can be powerful motivators for taking action. . . . Before you start to assemble your own plan and lessons to follow, think about what you want. . . . Don't hold back. Let your dream evolve. Most people have to learn how to dream again. When you were young, dreams were a natural process. Try to reestablish your ability to dream. Practice, practice, practice dreaming each day.

THE PRINCIPLE OF PASSION

Although having a vision is a good place to start, it is simply not enough. You must be absolutely *passionate* about that vision. To be passionate about a vision, an idea, or a cause means that you feel very strongly about it. You believe in that idea or vision with every fiber of your soul. In fact, you feel so strongly about your vision or your dream that you are compelled to act on it. It is that level of enthusiastic belief in a principle or idea that will enable you to be successful.

A vision often starts as an idea or strong belief in something. Over time it begins to take shape. The vision becomes more distinct and pronounced and as it does, your feelings about it begin to intensify. They become so strong, in fact, that you begin to pursue your dream with a passionate and zealous fervor. Jim "Mattress Mack" McIngvale is a perfect example of one who pursues his dreams with great passion. In *Always Think Big*, Jim asserts,

> My plan and dedication to success was burning and passionate. I would sell furniture, move furniture around, help deliver furniture, treat customers like royalty, and think up ways to outsell the competition. . . . I spent

every minute selling, selling, selling. Each day required 100 percent focus on and attention to customers. . . . I had a powerful desire and determination to succeed. What I possessed was deeper than a goal or destination. I had a determination to be successful.

One of the benefits of being passionate about your vision is that the enthusiasm you exert is often contagious. If you believe with all your heart and soul in what you are trying to accomplish, that belief will begin to be shared by others. When you are passionate about your dreams, your actions tend to reflect a level of zeal and fervor that others can't help but notice. Although many of your associates will share your beliefs, there are those who will have no interest whatsoever in your ideas. While it is okay to share your vision with others, be careful not to impose it on them. Writing of his own personal experience, Jim affirms,

One thing I learned through reading and observation is that there is a degree of fanaticism in some individuals that allows passion to actively destroy them in the long run. . . . Over the years I have learned to back off when others are smothered by my passion and determination. . . . I finally learned that not everyone can work at my pace. So what? As long as they treat customers right, delight them, and give Gallery their best, I can live with it. It took me years to learn the lesson that everyone is different and to respect these differences.

I encourage you to adapt the second principle of power, the principle of passion, in your pursuit of success. Believe with all of your heart, might, mind, and soul in the principles for which you stand. Transform your enthusiasm into determination and focused action tempered by respect for others. The fervent application of this principle has propelled many individuals to success. The principle of passion can help you to achieve your dreams.

THE PRINCIPLE OF AUTONOMY

The principle of autonomy is a crucial component of the three principles of power and is necessary to carry out and implement the first two, the principles of vision and of passion. Autonomy has to do with your ability to think and *act* independently of what others may think of you or your ideas. While it is imperative that you have a vision and are passionate about that vision, you must be confident enough within yourself to carry out that vision regardless of what others may say.

There are and will always be the naysayers of the world who will tell you that what you are trying to achieve simply cannot be done. They know because they have tried to do the same thing and have failed. This is not to suggest that you completely disregard what other people have to say. You should always be open-minded and welcome the input of others. To be autonomous, however, means that you are capable of making up your own mind. You listen to the suggestions of others, objectively evaluate the information, and then determine what course of action best fits your needs. In *Always Think Big,* Jim McIngvale describes the approach of traditional furniture establishments in delivering furniture and how he was told time after time that his vision of "buy it today and we'll deliver it tonight" would never work. In *Always Think Big,* Jim writes,

> Our competitors doubted that we could stick with the same day delivery approach. Gallery did, and we continue to prove them wrong. We enjoy being able to occasionally beat the customer to their home with their new furniture. Even today the Gallery delivery truck is waiting for some of our customers as they pull up to their homes. What a treat!

There you have it. Time after time, Jim McIngvale's competitors told him that it just couldn't be done. No one had succeeded in doing it before, and Gallery Furniture wouldn't be able to do it now. If Jim had listened to all the well-respected so-called experts in the furniture industry, he never would have succeeded in his dream to build the largest and most successful furniture store in Houston. As it turns out, Jim was able to far surpass his original goal by building the most successful furniture store in the world!

The third principle of power, the principle of autonomy, is vital to your success in real estate. You must be able to think and act independently of what others may advise. Don't be afraid to stand up for what you so passionately believe in—your visions, your dreams, your aspirations. Business acquaintances, friends, and even family members will tell you that it "just simply can't be done." I encourage you to politely ignore their pessimistic remarks and exercise your own free will. The ability to act autonomously is what distinguishes a leader from a follower. You already have the seed of leadership within you. Now you must water it and nourish it. You can do that by standing up for the principles you so firmly believe in. As you do, your leadership skills will grow, enabling you to achieve your goals. Jim "Mattress Mack" McIngvale offers this sage advice to those who dare to pursue their dreams in spite of what others may say.

> The principle of thinking big should be another part of your personal plan. . . . If you believe that your body is what it is fed, so is your mind. If your mind only thinks small or is uncertain, then you will act accordingly. In addition to doing the necessary small things, you should also think big and think bold. Telling me that it was impossible to adhere to my promise of same day delivery was like a jump start to me. Instead of accepting the naysayers' views about furniture delivery, I made up my mind to prove the doubters wrong. I never doubted that Gallery could be the business that brings same day delivery into the furniture industry. I refused to accept the noise coming at me for being "foolish," a "huckster," and "crazy dreamer."
>
> Surrendering to the doubters and naysayers would have been easy. Surrendering or changing my big dream was never an option. The pessimistic, negative, can't-do-it thinking of others required me to focus, pay attention to

details, and to work around the clock. To me, pessimism, small thinking, and ridicule are poisons to be avoided.

In summary, adapting the three principles of power into your real estate investment strategy can mean the difference between success and failure. First, you must have a clear and distinct vision of what you want to achieve. While your vision may lack clarity and detail initially, remember that as you work toward fulfilling it, the vision will eventually become crystal clear as you draw closer to accomplishing it. Once again, in the words of Zig Ziglar, "Go as far as you can see, and when you get there, you can always see farther." Second, you must be passionate about your dreams and aspirations to be successful. Your passion and enthusiasm for your dreams demonstrate to others your level of commitment. Pursuing your vision with passion and zeal is a manifestation to them that you are indeed determined to succeed. Finally, you must be able to act autonomously. You must break the shackles of dependence that so easily bind the commoners. You have the power to set yourself free! By incorporating the three principles of power—vision, passion, and autonomy—into your life, you will not only be able to achieve your goals, but you will be able to far surpass them. Implementing these principles will enable you to attain the highest level of achievement of which you are capable. You will be empowered to fulfill the measure of your creation, to reach your true potential, and to enjoy the generous gifts life has to offer. Your capacity to soar to magnificent heights far beyond the reach of the general masses will become infinite in scope, unlimited in magnitude, and vastly immeasurable by ordinary standards. You have the power within you to create your destiny. I encourage you to apply these principles in your life, for, by doing so, you will not only be able to create your destiny, you will also be able to fulfill it.

> **What lies behind us and what lies before us are small matters compared to what lies within us.**
> —*Ralph Waldo Emerson*

APPENDIX A

PROPERTY INSPECTION CHECKLIST

Date _____

Property Information: Seller's Name
                               Address
                               Phone Number

For the Project: Project Name
                               Address
                               Other Information

INSTRUCTIONS: Inspect the project and carefully check whether all items meet the project specifications. Initial in the space marked Satisfactory if the item meets with your approval. If an item is not satisfactory, describe the problem in the Comments field. Add additional information where necessary. Modify the list to fit your finish schedule. After work on the noted items has been completed, you will need to make a second inspection and initial in the last box for final approval.

■ Appendix A ■

Item	Satisfactory	Comments	Est Cost
Foyer			
Floors			
Ceilings			
Walls			
Light fixtures			
Windows			
Doors			
Trim moldings			
Other			
Dining Room			
Floors			
Ceilings			
Walls			
Light fixtures			
Windows			
Doors			
Trim moldings			
Other			
Living Room			
Floors			
Ceilings			
Walls			
Woodwork			
Light fixtures			
Windows			
Doors			

Initialed by: Buyer __ Seller __

Item	Satisfactory	Comments	Est Cost
Trim moldings			
Fireplace			
Other			
Kitchen			
Floors			
Ceilings			
Walls			
Light fixtures			
Windows			
Doors			
Trim moldings			
Cabinets			
Countertop			
Sink			
Oven and range			
Hood and exhaust fan			
Microwave			
Dishwasher			
Disposal			
Trash compactor			
Other			
Breakfast Room			
Floors			
Ceilings			
Walls			
Light fixtures			
Windows			

Initialed by: Buyer __ Seller __

Item	Satisfactory	Comments	Est Cost
Doors			
Trim moldings			
Other			
Family Room			
Floors			
Ceilings			
Walls			
Light fixtures			
Windows			
Doors			
Trim moldings			
Woodwork			
Other			
Powder Room			
Floors			
Ceilings			
Walls			
Light fixtures			
Windows			
Doors			
Trim moldings			
Vanity			
Toilet			
Towel bar			
Paper holder			
Other			

Initialed by: Buyer __ Seller __

■ Appendix A ■

Item	Satisfactory	Comments	Est Cost
Utility Room			
Floors			
Ceilings			
Walls			
Light fixtures			
Windows			
Doors			
Trim moldings			
Hot water heater			
Furnace/heat pump			
Washer hookup			
Dryer hookup			
Other			
Master Bedroom			
Floors			
Ceilings			
Walls			
Light fixtures			
Windows			
Doors			
Trim moldings			
Other			
Master Bath			
Floors			
Ceilings			

Initialed by: Buyer __ Seller __

Item	Satisfactory	Comments	Est Cost
Walls			
Light fixtures			
Windows			
Doors			
Trim moldings			
Vanity			
Toilet			
Whirlpool/garden tub			
Shower			
Shower door			
Towel bar			
Paper holder			
Other			
Bedroom 2			
Floors			
Ceilings			
Walls			
Light fixtures			
Windows			
Doors			
Trim moldings			
Other			
Bedroom 3			
Floors			
Ceilings			
Walls			
Light fixtures			

Initialed by: Buyer __ Seller __

Item	Satisfactory	Comments	Est Cost
Windows			
Doors			
Trim moldings			
Other			
Bedroom 4			
Floors			
Ceilings			
Walls			
Light fixtures			
Windows			
Doors			
Trim moldings			
Other			
Bedroom 5			
Floors			
Ceilings			
Walls			
Light fixtures			
Windows			
Doors			
Trim moldings			
Other			
Bath 2			
Floors			

Initialed by: Buyer __ Seller __

Item	Satisfactory	Comments	Est Cost
Ceilings			
Walls			
Light fixtures			
Windows			
Doors			
Trim moldings			
Vanity			
Toilet			
Shower			
Shower door			
Towel bar			
Paper holder			
Other			
Bath 3			
Floors			
Ceilings			
Walls			
Light fixtures			
Windows			
Doors			
Trim moldings			
Vanity			
Toilet			
Whirlpool/garden tub			
Shower			
Shower door			
Towel bar			
Paper holder			
Other			

Initialed by: Buyer __ Seller __

■ Appendix A ■

Item	Satisfactory	Comments	Est Cost
Bath 4			
Floors			
Ceilings			
Walls			
Light fixtures			
Windows			
Doors			
Trim moldings			
Vanity			
Toilet			
Whirlpool/garden tub			
Shower			
Shower door			
Towel bar			
Paper holder			
Other			
Hallway			
Floors			
Ceilings			
Walls			
Light fixtures			
Windows			
Doors			
Trim moldings			
Other			

Initialed by: Buyer __ Seller __

Item	Satisfactory	Comments	Est Cost
Garage			
Floors			
Ceilings			
Walls			
Light fixtures			
Windows			
Doors			
Trim moldings			
Garage door			
Garage door opener			
Storage area			
Other			
Study / Library			
Floors			
Ceilings			
Walls			
Light fixtures			
Windows			
Doors			
Trim moldings			
Other			
Additional Room			
Floors			
Ceilings			
Walls			
Light fixtures			
Windows			

Initialed by: Buyer __ Seller __

▪ Appendix A ▪

Item	Satisfactory	Comments	Est Cost
Doors			
Trim moldings			
Other			
Exterior			
Paint			
Exterior veneer			
Chimney			
Roof			
Doors			
Walkways			
Driveway			
Light fixtures			
Outlets			
Vents, dryer, fans, etc.			
Deck			
Porches			
Brick			
Siding			
Other			
HVAC Equipment			
Furnace			
Air conditioner			
Filters			
Ducts and vents			
Other			
Electrical			
Outlets			

Initialed by: Buyer __ Seller __

Item	Satisfactory	Comments	Est Cost
Wall switches			
Wiring			
Breaker panel			
Circuit breakers			
Other			
Foundation			
Concrete slab			
Basement			
Cracks			
Settling			
Evidence of leaks			
Mold or mildew			
Other			

FIRST INSPECTION

Having inspected the project listed herein, except for those specific items listed above, the Buyer accepts the project as is, in satisfactory condition and understands the Buyer will not have a claim against the Seller for any overlooked items not listed above that could have been seen in the Buyer's inspection. The Buyer has discussed the specific items with the Seller and understands that the Seller makes no guarantees or warranties other than those that are stated in the contract documents.

Seller's Signature   Date

Buyer's Signature   Date

Initialed by: Buyer __ Seller __

APPENDIX B

OWNER AND SUBCONTRACTOR AGREEMENT

THIS AGREEMENT, Made as of January 2, in the Year of 2004.

Between the Owner:	Mr. H. A. Stephens
	1234 N. Main St.
	(555) 555-5555
And the Subcontractor:	Cool's Air Conditioning Service
	License #123456
	1234 S. Main St.
	(555) 555-4444
For the Project:	Sample A/C Project
	4321 E. Main St.

ARTICLE 1. SCOPE OF WORK

1.1 Subcontractor has heretofore entered into a contract with said Owner to furnish all labor, materials and equipment to perform all work described below according to the construction documents.

Initialed by: Buyer __ Seller __

ARTICLE 2.   PAYMENT TERMS

2.1   The Owner agrees to pay the Subcontractor within 14 days after the completion of the work and payment by the owner for such work.

2.2   Subcontractor understands and agrees that progress payment requests shall be written and given to the owner before Wednesday for payment on the following Friday. All work for the portion requested must be completed prior to the request for payment. The Owner will request a draw and payment will be made to the Subcontractor after the draw is received. Please note that a certificate of Workmen's Compensation Insurance must be received before the first payment is made or the Owner will hold a percentage needed to cover the labor portion of the job.

2.3   The Total Contract Amount shall be $3687.00

ARTICLE 3.   TIME OF COMPLETION

3.1   Subcontractor shall keep both an adequate size and properly trained crew on the job site so as to complete the project within 30 days and work within the project schedule.

ARTICLE 4.   CHANGE ORDERS

4.1   Subcontractor understands and agrees that no change orders or contract additions will be made unless agreed to in writing by Owner. If any additional work is performed and not covered in this contract, the Subcontractor proceeds at his own risk and expense. No alterations, additions, or small changes can be made in the work or method of the performance, without the written change order signed by the owner and Subcontractor.

Initialed by: Buyer __ Seller __

ARTICLE 5. CLEANUP

5.1 Subcontractor will be responsible for cleaning up the job on a daily basis, including all generated construction debris, drink cans, food wrappers, and/or other trash. If it becomes necessary, the Subcontractor will be back-charged for appropriate cleanup by deducting cleanup costs from payments.

ARTICLE 6. TAXES AND PERMITS

6.1 The Subcontractor understands and agrees to be responsible for all taxes, fees, and expenses imposed directly or indirectly for its work, labor, material, and services required to fulfill this contract. The Subcontractor is responsible for all permits pertaining to the law, ordinances, and regulations where the work is performed.

ARTICLE 7. INSURANCE

7.1 The Subcontractor shall maintain, at his own expense, full and complete insurance on its work until final approval of the work described in the contract. The Subcontractor shall not hold the Owner liable for any and all costs, damages, fees, and expenses from any claims arising on the project. Failure of the Subcontractor to maintain appropriate insurance coverage may deem a material breach, allowing the Owner to terminate this contract or to provide insurance at the Subcontractor's expense.

ARTICLE 8. LIQUIDATED DAMAGES

8.1 If the project is not substantially completed on the stated completion date, the Subcontractor shall pay to the Owner the

Initialed by: Buyer __ Seller __

sum of $100 per day for each calendar day of inexcusable delay until the work is substantially completed, as liquidated damages.

ARTICLE 9.   WARRANTY

9.1   Subcontractor shall warranty all labor, materials, and equipment furnished on the project for one year against defects in workmanship or materials utilized. The manufacturer's warranty will prevail. No legal action of any kind relating to the project, project performance, or this contract shall be initiated by either party against the other party after five years beyond the completion of the project or cessation of work.

ARTICLE 10.   HAZARDOUS MATERIALS, WASTE, AND ASBESTOS

10.1   Both parties agree that dealing with hazardous materials, waste, or asbestos requires specialized training, processes, precautions, and licenses. Therefore, unless the scope of this agreement includes the specific handling, disturbance, removal, or transportation of hazardous materials, waste, or asbestos, upon discovery of such hazardous materials the Subcontractor shall notify the Owner immediately and allow the Owner to contract with a properly licensed and qualified hazardous material owner.

ARTICLE 11.   ARBITRATION OF DISPUTES

11.1   Any controversy or claim arising out of or relating to this contract, or the breach thereof, shall be settled by arbitration administered by the American Arbitration Association under its Construction Industry Arbitration Rules, and judgment on the award rendered by the arbitrator(s) may be entered in any court having jurisdiction thereof.

Initialed by: Buyer __ Seller __

ARTICLE 12.   ATTORNEY FEES

12.1   In the event of any arbitration or litigation relating to the project, project performance or this contract, the prevailing party shall be entitled to reasonable attorney fees, costs, and expenses.

ARTICLE 13.   ACCEPTANCE

WITNESS our hand and seal on this _____ day of _____, 20__.

Signed in the presence of:

_____   _____

Owner's Name   **Date**

_____   _____

Subcontractor's Name   **Date**

Appendix C

Sample Real Estate Forms

■ Appendix C ■

APPROVED BY THE TEXAS REAL ESTATE COMMISSION (TREC)   10-25-93

SELLER'S DISCLOSURE OF PROPERTY CONDITION

(SECTION 5.008, TEXAS PROPERTY CODE)

CONCERNING THE PROPERTY AT_____

(Street Address and City)

THIS NOTICE IS A DISCLOSURE OF SELLER'S KNOWLEDGE OF THE CONDITION OF THE PROPERTY AS OF THE DATE SIGNED BY SELLER AND IS NOT A SUBSTITUTE FOR ANY INSPECTIONS OR WARRANTIES THE PURCHASER MAY WISH TO OBTAIN. IT IS NOT A WARRANTY OF ANY KIND BY SELLER OR SELLER'S AGENTS.

Seller ☐ is ☐ is not occupying the Property. If unoccupied, how long since Seller has occupied the Property? _____

1. The Property has the items checked below [Write Yes (Y), No (N), or Unknown (U)]:

__Range	__Oven	__Microwave
__Dishwasher	__Trash Compactor	__Disposal
__Washer/Dryer Hookups	__Window Screens	__Rain Gutters
__Security System	__Fire Detection Equipment	__Intercom System
__TV Antenna	__Cable TV Wiring	__Satellite Dish
__Ceiling Fan(s)	__Attic Fan(s)	__Exhaust Fan(s)
__Central A/C	__Central Heating	__Wall/Window Air Conditioning
__Plumbing System	__Septic System	__Public Sewer System
__Patio/Decking	__Outdoor Grill	__Fences
__Pool	__Sauna	__Spa__Hot Tub
__Pool Equipment	__Pool Heater	__Automatic Lawn Sprinkler System
__Fireplace(s) & Chimney(Woodburning)	__Fireplace(s) & Chimney (Mock)	__Gas Lines (Nat./LP)
__Gas Fixtures	Garage:__Attached __Not Attached	__Carport
Garage Door Opener(s):	__Electronic	__Control(s)
Water Heater:	__Gas	__Electric
Water Supply: __City	__Well __MUD	__Co-op

Roof Type:_____   Age:_____(approx)

Are you (Seller) aware of any of the above items that are not in working condition, that have known defects, or that are in need of repair? ☐ Yes ☐ No ☐ Unknown. If yes, then describe. (Attach additional sheets if necessary): _____

_____

2. Are you (Seller) aware of any known defects/malfunctions in any of the following? Write Yes (Y) if you are aware, write No (N) if you are not aware.

__Interior Walls	__Ceilings	__Floors
__Exterior Walls	__Doors	__Windows
__Roof	__Foundation/Slab(s)	__Basement
__Walls/Fences	__Driveways	__Sidewalks
__Plumbing/Sewers/Septics	__Electrical Systems	__Lighting Fixtures
__Other Structural Components (Describe) _____		

01A   TREC No. OP-H

■ Appendix C ■

(Street Address and City)

If the answer to any of the above is yes, explain. (Attach additional sheets if necessary): _____

_____

_____

3. Are you (Seller) aware of any of the following conditions? Write Yes (Y) if you are aware, write No (N) if you are not aware.

___Active Termites (includes wood-   ___Termite or Wood Rot Damage   ___Previous Termite Damage
    destroying insects)   Needing Repair

___Previous Termite Treatment   ___Previous Flooding   ___Improper Drainage

___Water Penetration   ___Located in 100-Year Floodplain   ___Present Flood Insurance
                                                                            Coverage

___Previous Structural or Roof   ___Hazardous or Toxic Waste   ___Asbestos Components
    Repair

___Urea-formaldehyde Insulation   ___Radon Gas   ___Lead Based Paint
___Aluminum Wiring   ___Previous Fires   ___Unplatted Easements
___Landfill, Settling, Soil   ___Subsurface Structure or Pits
    Movement, Fault Lines

If the answer to any of the above is yes, explain. (Attach additional sheets if necessary): _____

_____

_____

4. Are you (Seller) aware of any item, equipment, or system in or on the Property that is in need of repair? ☐ Yes (if
you are aware) ☐ No (if you are not aware). If yes, explain (attach additional sheets as necessary). _____

_____

_____

5. Are you (Seller) aware of any of the following? Write Yes (Y) if you are aware, write No (N) if you are not aware.

___   Room additions, structural modifications, or other alterations or repairs made without necessary permits or not in compliance
    with building codes in effect at that time.

___   Homeowners' Association or maintenance fees or assessments.

___   Any "common area" (facilities such as pools, tennis courts, walkways, or other areas) co-owned in undivided interest with
    others.

___   Any notices of violations of deed restrictions or governmental ordinances affecting the condition or use of the Property.

___   Any lawsuits directly or indirectly affecting the Property.

___   Any condition on the Property which materially affects the physical health or safety of an individual.

If the answer to any of the above is yes, explain. (Attach additional sheets if necessary): _____

_____

_____

_____

_____   _____   _____   _____
Date   Signature of Seller   Date   Signature of Seller

The undersigned purchaser hereby acknowledges receipt of the foregoing notice.

_____   _____   _____   _____
Date   Signature of Purchaser   Date   Signature of Purchaser

01A   TREC No. OP-H

■ Appendix C ■

PROMULGATED BY THE TEXAS REAL ESTATE COMMISSION (TREC)   9-22-97

EQUAL HOUSING OPPORTUNITY

ONE TO FOUR FAMILY RESIDENTIAL CONTRACT (RESALE)
ALL CASH, ASSUMPTION, THIRD PARTY CONVENTIONAL OR SELLER FINANCING
NOTICE: Not For Use For Condominium Transactions

1. **PARTIES:** _____ (Seller) agrees
to sell and convey to _____(Buyer) and Buyer
agrees to buy from Seller the property described below.

2. **PROPERTY:** Lot _____, Block _____, _____
Addition, City of _____, _____ County,
Texas, known as _____
(Address/Zip Code), or as described on attached exhibit, together with the following items, if any: curtains
and rods, draperies and rods, valances, blinds, window shades, screens, shutters, awnings, wall-to-wall
carpeting, mirrors fixed in place, ceiling fans, attic fans, mail boxes, television antennas and satellite dish
system with controls and equipment, permanently installed heating and air-conditioning units, window air-
conditioning units, built-in security and fire detection equipment, plumbing and lighting fixtures including
chandeliers, water softener, stove, built-in kitchen equipment, garage door openers with controls, built-in
cleaning equipment, all swimming pool equipment and maintenance accessories, shrubbery, landscaping,
permanently installed outdoor cooking equipment, built-in fireplace screens, artificial fireplace logs and
all other property owned by Seller and attached to the above described real property except the following
property which is not included: _____
_____
_____.

All property sold by this contract is called the "Property." The Property ❏ is ❏ is not subject to mandatory
membership in an owners' association. The TREC Addendum For Property Subject To Mandatory
Membership In An Owners' Association ❏ is ❏ is not attached.

3. **SALES PRICE:**
A. Cash portion of Sales Price payable by Buyer at closing . . . . $_____
B. Sum of all financing described below
   (excluding any private mortgage insurance [PMI] premium) . . . . $_____
C. Sales Price (Sum of A and B) . . . . $_____

4. **FINANCING:** Within _____ days after the effective date of this contract Buyer shall apply for all third party
financing or noteholder's approval of any assumption and make every reasonable effort to obtain financing
or assumption approval. Financing or assumption approval will be deemed to have been obtained when
the lender determines that Buyer has satisfied all of lender's financial requirements (those items relating
to Buyer's net worth, income and creditworthiness). If financing (including any financed PMI premium) or
assumption approval is not obtained within _____ days after the effective date hereof, this contract will
terminate and the earnest money will be refunded to Buyer. Each note to be executed hereunder must be
secured by vendor's and deed of trust liens.
The portion of Sales Price not payable in cash will be paid as follows: (Check applicable boxes below)
❏ A. THIRD PARTY FINANCING:
   ❏ (1)   This contract is subject to approval for Buyer of a third party first mortgage loan having a
           loan-to-value ratio not to exceed _____ % as established by such third party (excluding any
           financed PMI premium), due in full in _____ year(s), with interest not to exceed _____ %
           per annum for the first _____ year(s) of the loan. The loan will be ❏ with ❏ without PMI.

Initialed for identification by Buyer_____ and Seller_____   **01A**   TREC NO. 20-3

▪ Appendix C ▪

❑ (2) This contract is subject to approval for Buyer of a third party second mortgage loan having a loan-to-value ratio not to exceed _____ % as established by such third party (excluding any financed PMI premium), due in full in _____ year(s), with interest not to exceed _____ % per annum for the first _____ year(s) of the loan. The loan will be ❑ with ❑ without PMI.

❑ B. TEXAS VETERANS' HOUSING ASSISTANCE PROGRAM LOAN: This contract is subject to approval for Buyer of a Texas Veterans' Housing Assistance Program Loan (the Program Loan) of $_____ for a period of at least _____ years at the interest rate established by the Texas Veterans' Land Board at the time of closing.

❑ C. SELLER FINANCING: A promissory note from Buyer to Seller of $_____, bearing _____ % interest per annum, secured by vendor's and deed of trust liens, in accordance with the terms and conditions set forth in the attached TREC Seller Financing Addendum. If an owner policy of title insurance is furnished, Buyer shall furnish Seller with a mortgagee policy of title insurance.

❑ D. ASSUMPTION:

❑ (1) Buyer shall assume the unpaid principal balance of a first lien promissory note payable to _____ which unpaid balance at closing will be $ _____ . The total current monthly payment including principal, interest and any reserve deposits is $ _____ . Buyer's initial payment will be the first payment due after closing.

❑ (2) Buyer shall assume the unpaid principal balance of a second lien promissory note payable to _____ which unpaid balance at closing will be $ _____ . The total current monthly payment including principal, interest and any reserve deposits is $ _____ . Buyer's initial payment will be the first payment due after closing.

Buyer's assumption of an existing note includes all obligations imposed by the deed of trust securing the note.

If the unpaid principal balance(s) of any assumed loan(s) as of the Closing Date varies from the loan balance(s) stated above, the ❑ cash payable at closing ❑ Sales Price will be adjusted by the amount of any variance; provided, if the total principal balance of all assumed loans varies in an amount greater than $350.00 at closing, either party may terminate this contract and the earnest money will be refunded to Buyer unless the other party elects to eliminate the excess in the variance by an appropriate adjustment at closing. If the noteholder requires (a) payment of an assumption fee in excess of $_____ in D(1) above or $ _____ in D(2) above and Seller declines to pay such excess, or (b) an increase in the interest rate to more than _____ % in D(1) above, or _____ % in D(2) above, or (c) any other modification of the loan documents, Buyer may terminate this contract and the earnest money will be refunded to Buyer. A vendor's lien and deed of trust to secure assumption will be required which shall automatically be released on execution and delivery of a release by noteholder. If Seller is released from liability on any assumed note, the vendor's lien and deed of trust to secure assumption will not be required.

NOTICE TO BUYER: The monthly payments, interest rates or other terms of some loans may be adjusted by the lender at or after closing. If you are concerned about the possibility of future adjustments, do not sign the contract without examining the notes and deeds of trust.

NOTICE TO SELLER: Your liability to pay the note assumed by Buyer will continue unless you obtain a release of liability from the lender. If you are concerned about future liability, you should use the TREC Release of Liability Addendum.

❑ E. CREDIT APPROVAL ON ASSUMPTION OR SELLER FINANCING: Within _____ days after the effective date of this contract, Buyer shall deliver to Seller ❑ credit report ❑ verification of employment, including salary ❑ verification of funds on deposit in financial institutions ❑ current financial statement to establish Buyer's creditworthiness for assumption approval or seller financing and ❑ _____.

If Buyer's documentation is not delivered within the specified time, Seller may terminate this contract by notice to Buyer within 7 days after expiration of the time for delivery, and the earnest money will

Initialed for identification by Buyer_____and Seller_____   **01A**   TREC NO. 20-3

■ Appendix C ■

be paid to Seller. If this contract is not so terminated, Seller will be deemed to have accepted Buyer's credit. If the documentation is timely delivered, and Seller determines in Seller's sole discretion that Buyer's credit is unacceptable, Seller may terminate this contract by notice to Buyer within 7 days after expiration of the time for delivery and the earnest money will be refunded to Buyer. If Seller does not so terminate this contract, Seller will be deemed to have accepted Buyer's credit. Buyer hereby authorizes any credit reporting agency to furnish to Seller at Buyer's sole expense copies of Buyer's credit reports.

5. **EARNEST MONEY:** Buyer shall deposit $_____ as earnest money with _____
_____ at _____
(Address), as escrow agent, upon execution of this contract by both parties. Additional earnest money of $_____ must be deposited by Buyer with escrow agent on or before _____,
19_____. If Buyer fails to deposit the earnest money as required by this contract, Buyer will be in default.

6. **TITLE POLICY AND SURVEY:**
   ❏ A. TITLE POLICY: Seller shall furnish to Buyer at ❏ Seller's ❏ Buyer's expense an owner policy of title insurance (the Title Policy) issued by _____(the Title Company) in the amount of the Sales Price, dated at or after closing, insuring Buyer against loss under the provisions of the Title Policy, subject to the promulgated exclusions (including existing building and zoning ordinances) and the following exceptions:
   (1) Restrictive covenants common to the platted subdivision in which the Property is located.
   (2) The standard printed exception for standby fees, taxes and assessments.
   (3) Liens created as part of the financing described in Paragraph 4.
   (4) Utility easements created by the dedication deed or plat of the subdivision in which the Property is located.
   (5) Reservations or exceptions otherwise permitted by this contract or as may be approved by Buyer in writing.
   (6) The standard printed exception as to discrepancies, conflicts, shortages in area or boundary lines, encroachments or protrusions, or overlapping improvements.
   (7) The standard printed exception as to marital rights.
   (8) The standard printed exception as to waters, tidelands, beaches, streams, and related matters.
   Within 20 days after the Title Company receives a copy of this contract, Seller shall furnish to Buyer a commitment for title insurance (the Commitment) and, at Buyer's expense, legible copies of restrictive covenants and documents evidencing exceptions in the Commitment other than the standard printed exceptions. Seller authorizes the Title Company to mail or hand deliver the Commitment and related documents to Buyer at Buyer's address shown below. If the Commitment is not delivered to Buyer within the specified time, the time for delivery will be automatically extended up to 15 days. Buyer will have 7 days after the receipt of the Commitment to object in writing to matters disclosed in the Commitment.
   ❏ B. SURVEY: (Check one box only)
      ❏ (1) Within_____ days after Buyer's receipt of a survey furnished to a third-party lender at ❏ Seller's ❏ Buyer's expense, Buyer may object in writing to any matter shown on the survey which constitutes a defect or encumbrance to title.
      ❏ (2) Within_____ days after the effective date of this contract, Buyer may object in writing to any matter which constitutes a defect or encumbrance to title shown on a survey obtained by Buyer at Buyer's expense.
   The survey must be made by a Registered Professional Land Surveyor acceptable to the Title Company and any lender. Utility easements created by the dedication deed and plat of the subdivision in which the Property is located will not be a basis for objection.
   Buyer may object to existing building and zoning ordinances, items 6A(1) through (8) above and matters shown on the survey if Buyer determines that any such ordinance, items or matters prohibits the following use or activity: _____
   _____

Initialed for identification by Buyer_____ and Seller_____   **01A**   TREC NO. 20-3

■ Appendix C ■

Buyer's failure to object under Paragraph 6A or 6B within the time allowed will constitute a waiver of Buyer's right to object; except that the requirements in Schedule C of the Commitment will not be deemed to have been waived. Seller shall cure the timely objections of Buyer or any third party lender within 15 days from the date Seller receives the objections and the Closing Date will be extended as necessary. If objections are not cured by the extended Closing Date, this contract will terminate and the earnest money will be refunded to Buyer unless Buyer elects to waive the objections.

NOTICE TO SELLER AND BUYER:

(1) Broker advises Buyer to have an abstract of title covering the Property examined by an attorney of Buyer's selection, or Buyer should be furnished with or obtain a Title Policy. If a Title Policy is furnished, the Commitment should be promptly reviewed by an attorney of Buyer's choice due to the time limitations on Buyer's right to object.

(2) If the Property is situated in a utility or other statutorily created district providing water, sewer, drainage, or flood control facilities and services, Chapter 49 of the Texas Water Code requires Seller to deliver and Buyer to sign the statutory notice relating to the tax rate, bonded indebtedness, or standby fee of the district prior to final execution of this contract.

(3) If the Property abuts the tidally influenced waters of the state, Section 33.135, Texas Natural Resources Code, requires a notice regarding coastal area property to be included in the contract. An addendum either promulgated by TREC or required by the parties should be used.

(4) Buyer is advised that the presence of wetlands, toxic substances, including asbestos and wastes or other environmental hazards or the presence of a threatened or endangered species or its habitat may affect Buyer's intended use of the Property. If Buyer is concerned about these matters, an addendum either promulgated by TREC or required by the parties should be used.

(5) Unless expressly prohibited in writing by the parties, Seller may continue to show the Property for sale and to receive, negotiate and accept back up offers.

(6) Any residential service contract that is purchased in connection with this transaction should be reviewed for the scope of coverage, exclusions and limitations. **The purchase of a residential service contract is optional. Similar coverage may be purchased from various companies authorized to do business in Texas.**

7. PROPERTY CONDITION:

A. INSPECTIONS, ACCESS AND UTILITIES: Buyer may have the Property inspected by an inspector selected by Buyer, licensed by TREC or otherwise permitted by law to make such inspections. Seller shall permit access to the Property at reasonable times for inspection, repairs and treatment and for reinspection after repairs and treatment have been completed. Seller shall pay for turning on utilities for inspection and reinspection.

B. SELLER'S DISCLOSURE NOTICE PURSUANT TO SECTION 5.008, TEXAS PROPERTY CODE (Notice) (check one box only):
   ❑ (1) Buyer has received the Notice.
   ❑ (2) Buyer has not received the Notice. Within _____ days after the effective date of this contract, Seller shall deliver the Notice to Buyer. If Buyer does not receive the Notice, Buyer may terminate this contract at any time prior to the closing. If Seller delivers the Notice, Buyer may terminate this contract for any reason within 7 days after Buyer receives the Notice or prior to the closing, whichever first occurs.
   ❑ (3) The Texas Property Code does not require this Seller to furnish the Notice.

C. SELLER'S DISCLOSURE OF LEAD-BASED PAINT AND LEAD-BASED PAINT HAZARDS is required by Federal law for a residential dwelling constructed prior to 1978. An addendum providing such disclosure ❑ is ❑ is not attached.

D. ACCEPTANCE OF PROPERTY CONDITION: (check one box only):
   ❑ (1) In addition to any earnest money deposited with escrow agent, Buyer has paid Seller $_____ (the "Option Fee") for the unrestricted right to terminate this contract by giving notice of termination to Seller within _____ days after the effective date of this contract. If Buyer gives notice of termination within the time specified, the Option Fee will not be refunded, however, any earnest money will be refunded to Buyer. If Buyer does not give notice of

Initialed for identification by Buyer_____ and Seller_____   **01A**   TREC NO. 20-3

■ Appendix C ■

One to Four Family Residential Contract Concerning_____Page Five 9-22-97

(Address of Property)

termination within the time specified, Buyer will be deemed to have accepted the Property in its current condition and the Option Fee ❏ will ❏ will not be credited to the Sales Price at closing.

❏ (2) Buyer accepts the Property in its present condition; provided Seller, at Seller's expense, shall complete the following repairs and treatment: _____

_____

_____.

E. LENDER REQUIRED REPAIRS AND TREATMENTS (REPAIRS): Unless otherwise agreed in writing, neither party is obligated to pay for lender required repairs or treatments for wood destroying insects. If the cost of lender required repairs exceeds 5% of the Sales Price, Buyer may terminate this contract.

F. COMPLETION OF REPAIRS AND TREATMENT. Unless otherwise agreed by the parties in writing, Seller shall complete all agreed repairs and treatment prior to the Closing Date. Repairs and treatments must be performed by persons who regularly provide such repairs or treatments. At Buyer's election, any transferable warranties received by Seller with respect to the repairs will be transferred to Buyer at Buyer's expense. If Seller fails to complete any agreed repairs and treatment prior to the Closing Date, Buyer may do so and the Closing Date will be extended up to 15 days, if necessary, to complete repairs and treatment or treatments for wood destroying insects.

8. **BROKERS' FEES:** All obligations of the parties for payment of brokers' fees are contained in separate written agreements.

9. **CLOSING:** The closing of the sale will be on or before _____, 19____, or within 7 days after objections to matters disclosed in the Commitment or by the survey have been cured, whichever date is later (the Closing Date). *If financing or assumption approval has been obtained pursuant to Paragraph 4,* the Closing Date will be extended up to 15 days if necessary to comply with lender's closing requirements (for example, appraisal, survey, insurance policies, lender-required repairs, closing documents). If either party fails to close this sale by the Closing Date, the non-defaulting party will be entitled to exercise the remedies contained in Paragraph 15. At closing Seller shall furnish tax statements or certificates showing no delinquent taxes and a general warranty deed conveying good and indefeasible title showing no additional exceptions to those permitted in Paragraph 6.

10. **POSSESSION:** Seller shall deliver possession of the Property to Buyer on _____ in its present or required repaired condition, ordinary wear and tear excepted. Any possession by Buyer prior to closing or by Seller after closing which is not authorized by a temporary lease form promulgated by TREC or required by the parties will establish a tenancy at sufferance relationship between the parties. *Consult your insurance agent prior to change of ownership or possession as insurance coverage may be limited or terminated. The absence of a written lease or appropriate insurance coverage may expose the parties to economic loss.*

11. **SPECIAL PROVISIONS:** (Insert only factual statements and business details applicable to this sale. TREC rules prohibit licensees from adding factual statements or business details for which a contract addendum, lease or other form has been promulgated by TREC for mandatory use.)

Initialed for identification by Buyer_____ and Seller_____   **01A**   TREC NO. 20-3

■ Appendix C ■

(Address of Property)

12. SETTLEMENT AND OTHER EXPENSES:

A. The following expenses must be paid at or prior to closing:

(1) Appraisal fees will be paid by _____.

(2) The total of loan discount fees (including any Texas Veterans' Housing Assistance Program Participation Fee) may not exceed _____% of the loan of which Seller shall pay _____ and Buyer shall pay the remainder. The total of any buydown fees may not exceed _____ which will be paid by _____.

(3) Seller's Expenses: Releases of existing liens, including prepayment penalties and recording fees; release of Seller's loan liability; tax statements or certificates; preparation of deed; one-half of escrow fee; and other expenses stipulated to be paid by Seller under other provisions of this contract.

(4) Buyer's Expenses: Loan application, origination and commitment fees; loan assumption costs; preparation and recording of deed of trust to secure assumption; lender required expenses incident to new loans, including PMI premium, preparation of loan documents, loan related inspection fee, recording fees, tax service and research fees, warehouse or underwriting fees, copies of restrictions and easements, amortization schedule, premiums for mortgagee title policies and endorsements required by lender, credit reports, photos; required premiums for flood and hazard insurance; required reserve deposit for insurance premiums and ad valorem taxes; interest on all monthly installment notes from date of disbursements to one month prior to dates of first monthly payments; customary Program Loan costs for Buyer; one-half of escrow fee; and other expenses stipulated to be paid by Buyer under other provisions of this contract.

B. If any expense exceeds an amount expressly stated in this contract for such expense to be paid by a party, that party may terminate this contract unless the other party agrees to pay such excess. In no event will Buyer pay charges and fees expressly prohibited by the Texas Veterans' Housing Assistance Program or other governmental loan program regulations.

13. PRORATIONS:
Taxes for the current year, interest, maintenance fees, assessments, dues and rents will be prorated through the Closing Date. If taxes for the current year vary from the amount prorated at closing, the parties shall adjust the prorations when tax statements for the current year are available. *If a loan is assumed* and the lender maintains an escrow account, the escrow account must be transferred to Buyer without any deficiency. Buyer shall reimburse Seller for the amount in the transferred account. Buyer shall pay the premium for a new insurance policy. If taxes are not paid at or prior to closing, Buyer will be obligated to pay taxes for the current year.

14. CASUALTY LOSS:
If any part of the Property is damaged or destroyed by fire or other casualty loss after the effective date of the contract, Seller shall restore the Property to its previous condition as soon as reasonably possible, but in any event by the Closing Date. If Seller fails to do so due to factors beyond Seller's control, Buyer may either (a) terminate this contract and the earnest money will be refunded to Buyer (b) extend the time for performance up to 15 days and the Closing Date will be extended as necessary or (c) accept the Property in its damaged condition and accept an assignment of insurance proceeds. Seller's obligations under this paragraph are independent of any obligations of Seller under Paragraph 7.

15. DEFAULT:
If Buyer fails to comply with this contract, Buyer will be in default, and Seller may either (a) enforce specific performance, seek such other relief as may be provided by law, or both, or (b) terminate this contract and receive the earnest money as liquidated damages, thereby releasing both parties from this contract. If, due to factors beyond Seller's control, Seller fails within the time allowed to make any non-casualty repairs or deliver the Commitment, Buyer may either (a) extend the time for performance up to 15 days and the Closing Date will be extended as necessary or (b) terminate this contract as the sole remedy and receive the earnest money. If Seller fails to comply with this contract for any other reason, Seller will be in default and Buyer may either (a) enforce specific performance, seek such other relief as may be provided by law, or both, or (b) terminate this contract and receive the earnest money, thereby releasing both parties from this contract.

▪ Appendix C ▪

16. **DISPUTE RESOLUTION:** It is the policy of the State of Texas to encourage the peaceable resolution of disputes through alternative dispute resolution procedures. The parties are encouraged to use an addendum approved by TREC to submit to mediation disputes which cannot be resolved in good faith through informal discussion.

17. **ATTORNEY'S FEES:** The prevailing party in any legal proceeding brought under or with respect to the transaction described in this contract is entitled to recover from the non-prevailing party all costs of such proceeding and reasonable attorney's fees.

18. **ESCROW:** The earnest money is deposited with escrow agent with the understanding that escrow agent is not (a) a party to this contract and does not have any liability for the performance or nonperformance of any party to this contract, (b) liable for interest on the earnest money and (c) liable for any loss of earnest money caused by the failure of any financial institution in which the earnest money has been deposited unless the financial institution is acting as escrow agent. At closing, the earnest money must be applied first to any cash down payment, then to Buyer's closing costs and any excess refunded to Buyer. If both parties make written demand for the earnest money, escrow agent may require payment of unpaid expenses incurred on behalf of the parties and a written release of liability of escrow agent from all parties. If one party makes written demand for the earnest money, escrow agent shall give notice of the demand by providing to the other party a copy of the demand. If escrow agent does not receive written objection to the demand from the other party within 30 days after notice to the other party, escrow agent may disburse the earnest money to the party making demand reduced by the amount of unpaid expenses incurred on behalf of the party receiving the earnest money and escrow agent may pay the same to the creditors. If escrow agent complies with the provisions of this paragraph, each party hereby releases escrow agent from all adverse claims related to the disbursal of the earnest money. Escrow agent's notice to the other party will be effective when deposited in the U. S. Mail, postage prepaid, certified mail, return receipt requested, addressed to the other party at such party's address shown below. Notice of objection to the demand will be deemed effective upon receipt by escrow agent.

19. **REPRESENTATIONS:** Seller represents that as of the Closing Date (a) there will be no liens, assessments, or security interests against the Property which will not be satisfied out of the sales proceeds unless securing payment of any loans assumed by Buyer and (b) assumed loans will not be in default. If any representation in this contract is untrue on the Closing Date, this contract may be terminated by Buyer and the earnest money will be refunded to Buyer. All representations contained in this contract will survive closing.

20. **FEDERAL TAX REQUIREMENT:** If Seller is a "foreign person," as defined by applicable law, or if Seller fails to deliver an affidavit that Seller is not a "foreign person," then Buyer shall withhold from the sales proceeds an amount sufficient to comply with applicable tax law and deliver the same to the Internal Revenue Service together with appropriate tax forms. IRS regulations require filing written reports if cash in excess of specified amounts is received in the transaction.

21. **AGREEMENT OF PARTIES:** This contract contains the entire agreement of the parties and cannot be changed except by their written agreement. Addenda which are a part of this contract are (list): _____
_____
_____
_____
_____
_____ .

22. **CONSULT YOUR ATTORNEY:** Real estate licensees cannot give legal advice. This contract is intended to be legally binding. READ IT CAREFULLY. If you do not understand the effect of this contract, consult your attorney BEFORE signing.

Buyer's   Seller's
Attorney is:_____   Attorney is:_____

▪ Appendix C ▪

One to Four Family Residential Contract Concerning_____Page Eight   9-22-97
(Address of Property)

23. NOTICES: All notices from one party to the other must be in writing and are effective when mailed to, hand-delivered at, or transmitted by facsimile machine as follows:

To Buyer at: **To Seller at:**

_____   _____

_____   _____

_____   _____

Telephone:(   )_____   Telephone:(   )_____

Facsimile:(   )_____   Facsimile:(   )_____

EXECUTED the_____day of _____, 19____ (THE EFFECTIVE DATE). (BROKER: FILL IN THE DATE OF FINAL ACCEPTANCE.)

_____   _____
Buyer   Seller

_____   _____
Buyer   Seller

BROKER INFORMATION AND RATIFICATION OF FEE

Listing Broker has agreed to pay Other Broker _____ of the total sales price when Listing Broker's fee is received. Escrow Agent is authorized and directed to pay Other Broker from Listing Broker's fee at closing.

_____   _____
Other Broker   License No.   Listing Broker   License No.

represents ☐ Seller as Listing Broker's subagent   represents ☐ Seller and Buyer as an intermediary
            ☐ Buyer only as Buyer's agent   ☐ Seller only as Seller's agent

                                       _____
                                       Listing Associate   Telephone

_____   _____
Associate   Telephone   Selling Associate   Telephone

_____   _____
Broker Address   Broker Address

                                       _____
                                       Telephone   Facsimile
_____
Telephone   Facsimile

RECEIPT

Receipt of ☐ Contract and ☐ $_____ Earnest Money in the form of_____is acknowledged.

Escrow Agent: _____   Date: _____, 19____

By:_____

_____   Telephone: (   )_____
Address
_____   Facsimile: (   )_____
City   State   Zip Code

01A   TREC NO. 20-3

▪ Appendix C ▪

10-29-01

PROMULGATED BY THE TEXAS REAL ESTATE COMMISSION (TREC)

THIRD PARTY FINANCING CONDITION ADDENDUM

TO CONTRACT CONCERNING THE PROPERTY AT

_____

(Street Address and City)

Buyer shall apply promptly for all financing described below and make every reasonable effort to obtain financing approval. Financing approval will be deemed to have been obtained when the lender determines that Buyer has satisfied all of lender's financial requirements (those items relating to Buyer's assets, income and credit history). If financing (including any financed PMI premium) approval is not obtained within _____ days after the effective date, this contract will terminate and the earnest money will be refunded to Buyer. Each note must be secured by vendor's and deed of trust liens.

CHECK APPLICABLE BOXES:

❑ A. CONVENTIONAL FINANCING:

    ❑ (1) A first mortgage loan in the principal amount of $ _____ (excluding any financed PMI premium), due in full in _____ year(s), with interest not to exceed _____% per annum for the first _____year(s) of the loan with Loan Fees not to exceed _____ % of the loan. The loan will be ❑ with ❑ without PMI.

    ❑ (2) A second mortgage loan in the principal amount of $_____(excluding any financed PMI premium), due in full in _____year(s), with interest not to exceed _____% per annum for the first _____year(s) of the loan with Loan Fees not to exceed _____ % of the loan. The loan will be ❑ with ❑ without PMI.

❑ B. TEXAS VETERANS' HOUSING ASSISTANCE PROGRAM LOAN: A Texas Veteran's Housing Assistance Program Loan of $_____ for a period of at least _____years at the interest rate established by the Texas Veteran's Land Board at the time of closing.

❑ C. FHA INSURED FINANCING: A Section _____ FHA insured loan of not less than $_____ (excluding any financed MIP), amortizable monthly for not less than _____years, with interest not to exceed _____% per annum for the first _____year(s) of the loan with Loan Fees not to exceed _____ % of the loan. As required by HUD-FHA, if FHA valuation is unknown, _It is expressly agreed that, notwithstanding any other provision of this contract, the purchaser (Buyer) shall not be obligated to complete the purchase of the Property described herein or to incur any penalty by forfeiture of earnest money deposits or otherwise unless the purchaser (Buyer) has been given in accordance with HUD/FHA or VA requirements a written statement issued by the Federal Housing Commissioner, Department of Veterans Affairs, or a Direct Endorsement Lender setting forth the appraised value of the Property of not less than $_____. The purchaser (Buyer) shall have the privilege and option of proceeding with consummation of the contract without regard to the amount of the appraised valuation. The appraised valuation is arrived at to determine the maximum mortgage the Department of Housing and Urban Development will insure. HUD does not warrant the value or the condition of the Property. The purchaser (Buyer) should satisfy himself/herself that the price and the condition of the Property are acceptable._

If the FHA appraised value of the Property (excluding closing costs and MIP) is less than the Sales Price, Seller may reduce the Sales Price to an amount equal to the FHA appraised value (excluding closing costs and MIP) and the sale will be closed at the lower Sales Price with proportionate adjustments to the down payment and loan amount.

Initialed for identification by Buyer_____ and Seller_____   **01A**

▪ Appendix C ▪

_____
(Address of Property)

❑ D. VA GUARANTEED FINANCING: A VA guaranteed loan of not less than $_____
(excluding any financed Funding Fee), amortizable monthly for not less than_____years,
with interest not to exceed_____% per annum for the first _____year(s) of the loan
with Loan Fees not to exceed _____ % of the loan.

VA NOTICE TO BUYER: "_It is expressly agreed that, notwithstanding any other provisions of
this contract, the Buyer shall not incur any penalty by forfeiture of earnest money or
otherwise or be obligated to complete the purchase of the Property described herein, if the
contract purchase price or cost exceeds the reasonable value of the Property established by
the Department of Veterans Affairs. The Buyer shall, however, have the privilege and
option of proceeding with the consummation of this contract without regard to the amount
of the reasonable value established by the Department of Veterans Affairs._"

If Buyer elects to complete the purchase at an amount in excess of the reasonable value
established by VA, Buyer shall pay such excess amount in cash from a source which Buyer
agrees to disclose to the VA and which Buyer represents will not be from borrowed funds
except as approved by VA. If VA reasonable value of the Property is less than the Sales
Price, Seller may reduce the Sales Price to an amount equal to the VA reasonable value and
the sale will be closed at the lower Sales Price with proportionate adjustments to the down
payment and the loan amount.

_____   _____
Buyer   Seller

_____   _____
Buyer   Seller

01A

PROMULGATED BY THE TEXAS REAL ESTATE COMMISSION (TREC)   10-29-01

SELLER FINANCING ADDENDUM
TO CONTRACT CONCERNING THE PROPERTY AT

_____

(Street Address and City)

A. CREDIT DOCUMENTATION. Within_____days after the effective date of this contract, Buyer shall deliver to Seller ❑ credit report ❑ verification of employment, including salary ❑ verification of funds on deposit in financial institutions ❑ current financial statement to establish Buyer's creditworthiness and ❑ _____.

Buyer hereby authorizes any credit reporting agency to furnish to Seller at Buyer's sole expense copies of Buyer's credit reports.

B. CREDIT APPROVAL. If Buyer's documentation is not delivered within the specified time, Seller may terminate this contract by notice to Buyer within 7 days after expiration of the time for delivery, and the earnest money will be paid to Seller. If the documentation is timely delivered, and Seller determines in Seller's sole discretion that Buyer's credit is unacceptable, Seller may terminate this contract by notice to Buyer within 7 days after expiration of the time for delivery and the earnest money will be refunded to Buyer. If Seller does not terminate this contract, Seller will be deemed to have accepted Buyer's credit.

C. PROMISSORY NOTE. The promissory note (Note) described in Paragraph 4 of this contract payable by Buyer to the order of Seller will be payable at the place designated by Seller. Buyer may prepay the Note in whole or in part at any time without penalty. Any prepayments are to be applied to the payment of the installments of principal last maturing and interest will immediately cease on the prepaid principal. The Note will contain a provision for payment of a late fee of 5% of any installment not paid within 10 days of the due date. The Note will be payable as follows:

❑ (1) In one payment due _____ after the date of the Note
with interest payable_____.

❑ (2) In _____ installments of $ _____ ❑ including interest
❑ plus interest beginning _____ after the date of the
Note and continuing at _____ intervals thereafter for _____when
the balance of the Note will be due and payable.

❑ (3) Interest only in _____ installments for the first _____ month(s)
and thereafter in installments of $_____ ❑ including interest ❑ plus
interest beginning _____ after the date of the Note and
continuing at _____ intervals thereafter for _____ when the
balance of the Note will be due and payable.

D. DEED OF TRUST. The deed of trust securing the Note will provide for the following:

(1) PROPERTY TRANSFERS: (check only one)

❑ (a) Consent Not Required: The Property may be sold, conveyed or leased without the consent of Seller, provided any subsequent buyer assumes the Note.

❑ (b) Consent Required: If all or any part of the Property is sold, conveyed, leased for a period longer than 3 years, leased with an option to purchase, or otherwise sold (including any contract for deed), without the prior written consent of Seller, Seller may declare the

Initialed for identification by Buyer_____ and Seller_____   **01A**

_____

(Address of Property)

balance of the Note, to be immediately due and payable. The creation of a subordinate lien, any conveyance under threat or order of condemnation, any deed solely between buyers, the passage of title by reason of the death of a buyer or by operation of law will not entitle Seller to exercise the remedies provided in this paragraph.

(2) TAX AND INSURANCE ESCROW: (check only one)

❑ (a) Escrow Not Required: Buyer shall furnish Seller annually, before the taxes become delinquent, evidence that all taxes on the Property have been paid. Buyer shall furnish Seller annually evidence of paid-up casualty insurance naming Seller as an additional loss payee.

❑ (b) Escrow Required: With each installment Buyer shall deposit with Seller in escrow a pro rata part of the estimated annual ad valorem taxes and casualty insurance premiums for the Property. Buyer shall pay any deficiency within 30 days after notice from Seller. Buyer's failure to pay the deficiency constitutes a default under the deed of trust. Buyer is not required to deposit any escrow payments for taxes and insurance that are deposited with a superior lienholder. The casualty insurance must name Seller as an additional loss payee.

(3) PRIOR LIENS: Any default under any lien superior to the lien securing the Note constitutes default under the deed of trust securing the Note.

_____   _____
Buyer   Seller

_____   _____
Buyer   Seller

01A

▪ Appendix C ▪

PROMULGATED BY THE TEXAS REAL ESTATE COMMISSION (TREC) 10-29-01

EQUAL HOUSING OPPORTUNITY

LOAN ASSUMPTION ADDENDUM
TO CONTRACT CONCERNING THE PROPERTY AT

_____
(Street Address and City)

A. CREDIT DOCUMENTATION. Within_____days after the effective date of this contract, Buyer shall deliver to Seller ❑ credit report ❑ verification of employment, including salary ❑ verification of funds on deposit in financial institutions ❑ current financial statement to establish Buyer's creditworthiness and ❑ _____
_____.
Buyer hereby authorizes any credit reporting agency to furnish to Seller at Buyer's sole expense copies of Buyer's credit reports.

B. CREDIT APPROVAL. If Buyer's documentation is not delivered within the specified time, Seller may terminate this contract by notice to Buyer within 7 days after expiration of the time for delivery, and the earnest money will be paid to Seller. If the documentation is timely delivered, and Seller determines in Seller's sole discretion that Buyer's credit is unacceptable, Seller may terminate this contract by notice to Buyer within 7 days after expiration of the time for delivery and the earnest money will be refunded to Buyer. If Seller does not terminate this contract, Seller will be deemed to have accepted Buyer's credit.

C. ASSUMPTION.

❑ (1) The unpaid principal balance of a first lien promissory note payable to _____
_____ which unpaid balance at closing will be $ _____. The total current monthly payment including principal, interest and any reserve deposits is $ _____. Buyer's initial payment will be the first payment due after closing.

❑ (2) The unpaid principal balance of a second lien promissory note payable to _____
_____ which unpaid balance at closing will be $ _____. The total current monthly payment including principal, interest and any reserve deposits is $ _____. Buyer's initial payment will be the first payment due after closing.

Buyer's assumption of an existing note includes all obligations imposed by the deed of trust securing the note. If the unpaid principal balance(s) of any assumed loan(s) as of the Closing Date varies from the loan balance(s) stated above, the ❑ cash payable at closing ❑ Sales Price will be adjusted by the amount of any variance; provided, if the total principal balance of all assumed loans varies in an amount greater than $350.00 at closing, either party may terminate this contract and the earnest money will be refunded to Buyer unless the other party elects to eliminate the excess in the variance by an appropriate adjustment at closing. Buyer may terminate this contract and the earnest money will be refunded to Buyer if the noteholder requires (a) payment of an assumption fee in excess of $ _____ in (1) above or $ _____ in (2) above and Seller declines to pay such excess, (b) an increase in the interest rate to more than _____% in (1) above, or _____% in (2) above, (c) any other modification of the loan documents, or (d) consent to the assumption of the loan and fails to consent. A vendor's lien and deed of trust to secure assumption will be required which will automatically be released on execution and delivery of a release by noteholder. If Seller is released from liability on any assumed note, the vendor's lien and deed of trust to secure assumption will not be required. If noteholder maintains an escrow account, the escrow account must be transferred to Buyer without any deficiency. Buyer shall reimburse Seller for the amount in the transferred accounts.

NOTICE TO BUYER: The monthly payments, interest rates or other terms of some loans may be adjusted by the noteholder at or after closing. If you are concerned about the possibility of future adjustments, do not sign the contract without examining the notes and deeds of trust.

NOTICE TO SELLER: Your liability to pay the note assumed by Buyer will continue unless you obtain a release of liability from the noteholder. If you are concerned about future liability, you should use the TREC Release of Liability Addendum.

_____   _____
Buyer   Seller

_____   _____
Buyer   Seller

01A

■ Appendix C ■

10-29-01

PROMULGATED BY THE TEXAS REAL ESTATE COMMISSION (TREC)

NOTICE OF TERMINATION OF CONTRACT

To: Seller(s)

In accordance with the unrestricted right of Buyer to terminate the contract between

_____

as Seller and _____

as Buyer dated _____, 20_____ for the Property located at _____

_____,

Buyer notifies Seller that the contract is terminated.

_____ _____
Buyer   Date   Buyer   Date

01A

Appendix D

Sample Personal Financial Statement

■ Appendix D ■

PERSONAL FINANCIAL STATEMENT

SECTION 1A: INDIVIDUAL INFORMATION		SECTION 1B: SPOUSAL INFORMATION	
Name:	Benjamin Investor	Name:	Barbara Investor
Residence:	123 North 2nd Street	Residence:	123 North 2nd Street
City, State, and Zip:	Anywhere, PA 12345	City, State, and Zip:	Anywhere, PA 12345
Position or Occupation Real Estate Investments		Position or Occupation Real Estate Investments	
Business Name:	Benjamin Real Estate Group	Business Name:	Benjamin Real Estate Group
Business Address:	456 East Main	Business Address:	456 East Main
City, State, and Zip:	Anywhere, PA 12345	City, State, and Zip:	Anywhere, PA 12345
Residence Phone: (212) 396-1234 Bus. Phone: (212) 396-1235		Residence Phone: (212) 396-1234 Bus. Phone: (212) 396-1235	
SSN:	123-45-6789 Date of Birth: 08/06/1959	SSN:	987-65-4321 Date of Birth: 08/06/1959
Driver's License #:	082812477	Driver's License #:	082812478

SECTION 2: BALANCE SHEET

ASSETS				LIABILITIES			
Cash (from Schedule 1)			313,000			Secured	10,155
Securities (from Schedule 2)	Marketable		275,300	Notes Payable to Banks (Sched 5)		Unsecured	72,665
	Nonmarketable		485,000			To Relatives	3,200
Notes and Accounts Receivable (Schedule 3)			50,000	Other Accounts and Notes Payable		To Others	0
Professional Accounts Receivable			42,000	Outstanding Credit Card Balances (Sched 6)			12,000
Real Estate (from Schedule 4)			405,000	Real Estate (from Schedule 4)			198,000
Cash Surrender Value Life Insurance			2,500			Income Taxes	0
Autos	Year: '96	Make: GM	11,500	Taxes Owed		Other Taxes	0
	Year: 2000	Make: Toy	16,000				
	Year:	Make:					
Oil Interests/Production Leases			4,200				
Personal Property/Household, etc.			145,000	Other Liabilities			
Other Assets (Itemize)	Computer Equipment		14,800	(Itemize)			
	Software & Peripherals		3,600				
	Jewelry		8,500				
				Total Liabilities			296,020
				Net Worth			1,480,380
TOTAL ASSETS			1,776,400	TOTAL LIABILITIES AND NET WORTH			1,776,400

CURRENT ANNUAL INCOME		CONTINGENT LIABILITIES			
Gross Annual Salary	82,000	As Endorser			
Bonuses and Commissions	16,000	As Guarantor			
Dividends and Interest	13,000	On Leases or Contracts			
Real Estate Income	145,000	Legal Claims or Judgments			
Oil Income	0	Provision for Federal Income Tax			
Other Income	1,500	Other (Itemize)			
TOTAL INCOME	257,500				

COMPARISON OF MONTHLY INCOME TO EXPENSES					
Net Monthly Income	21,458				
Rent or Home Payment	3,475	Have you ever declared bankruptcy?			
Food and Utilities	850	Yes		No	X
Incidentals, Travel, Insurance, etc.	1,400	If yes, please explain.			
Credit Cards and Loans	1,917				
TOTAL EXPENSES	7,642				
DISCRETIONARY INCOME	13,816				

The information contained in this statement is provided for the purpose of obtaining or maintaining credit on behalf of the undersigned or for the guarantee of debt by the undersigned. Each undersigned understands that the Bank is relying on the information provided herein (including the designation made as to the ownership of property) in deciding to grant or continue credit. Each undersigned represents and warrants that the information provided is true and complete and that the Bank may consider this statement as continuing to be true and correct until a written notice of a change is given to the Bank by the undersigned. I/we authorize the Bank to make all inquiries deemed necessary to verify the accuracy of the statements made herein, and to determine my/our credit worthiness. I/we authorize the Bank to answer questions about the Bank's credit experience with me/us.

Signature (Individual) _____

Date _____

Signature (Spouse) _____

Date _____

■ Appendix D ■

SECTION 3: SCHEDULES						

SCHEDULE 1: CASH IN BANKS AND OTHER INSTITUTIONS

Name and Location		Type of Account	Current Balance
ABC Federal Credit Union		Checking	4,500
My Favorite Bank		Money Market	210,000
E Bank		Savings	98,500
		TOTAL	313,000

SCHEDULE 2A: MARKETABLE SECURITIES/LIQUID ASSETS

Number of Shares	Description of Security	Cost	If Pledged, To Whom	Current Market Value
2,500	GOLD	12,500		28,000
5,000	DROOY	5,700		22,000
10,000	SSRI	18,900		29,800
4,500	Mutual Fund	45,000		48,500
	Precious Metals	125,000		147,000
			TOTAL	275,300

SCHEDULE 2B: NONMARKETABLE SECURITIES

Number of Shares	Description of Security	Cost	If Pledged, To Whom	Current Market Value
50% ownership	Symphony Homes, L.L.C.			485,000
			TOTAL	485,000

SCHEDULE 3: NOTES AND ACCOUNTS RECEIVABLE

Name and Address of Debtor	Is Debtor a Relative?	Origination Date	Nature or Description of Debt	Collateral Held	Final Payment Date	Current Balance
J.P. Smithers	No	02/01/2002	real estate loan	land	N/A	50,000
					TOTAL	50,000

SCHEDULE 4: REAL ESTATE, Legal & equitable title to real estate listed is solely in the name of undersigned unless otherwise noted.

Legal Description Or Street Address	Date Acquired	Type of Property	Mortgage or Lien Holder	Monthly Payments	Purchase Price	Remaining Loan Balance	Current Market Value
1234 Milcrest	06/01/1995	residence	Wells Fargo	800	147,500	70,000	265,000
5678 Angels Cove	07/01/1985	rental	None-1/2 interest	0	76,000	41,000	140,000
1234 Milcrest	12/10/2001	residence	Ntl City - HELOC	150		87,000	0
					TOTAL	198,000	405,000

SCHEDULE 5: NOTES PAYABLE

Holder's Name and Address	Original Amount	Date Opened	Collateral	Maturity Date	Monthly Payments	Current Balance
Larry Peabody	100,000	01/01/1998	unsecured line of cred	Open	742	44,265
GMAC	12,500	03/01/2000	GM auto	03/01/2004	245	10,155
SLAS - student loan	35,000	07/25/1992	none	07/25/2012	375	28,400
				TOTAL	1,362	82,820

SCHEDULE 6: CREDIT CARDS

Company's Name and Address	Credit Limit	Date Opened	Type (MC, Visa, Discover)	Maturity Date	Monthly Payments	Current Balance
Wells Fargo	2,500	04/08/1995	MC	Open	255	3,600
Citibank	15,000	09/09/1999	MC	Open	300	8,400
				TOTAL	555	12,000

APPENDIX E

WWW.THEVALUEPLAY.COM

Current ordering information for The Value Play Rehab Analyzer can be found at www.thevalueplay.com.

INSPIRATIONAL QUOTES AND STORIES

Although many of the inspirational quotes and stories are taken from the author's personal favorites and life experiences, material submitted by readers is welcomed. If you would like to submit one or more of your favorite inspirational quotes and/or stories for use in a future book, please visit the web site address located at www.thevalueplay.com. Anything submitted through this site will be considered by the author for possible future use. Proper credit will be given to contributors whose quotes or stories are used in future books.

APPENDIX F

WWW.SYMPHONY-HOMES.COM

For information regarding Symphony Homes, please log on to our web site at www.symphony-homes.com.

INDEX